SYSTEM BLUEPRINT

ULTIMATE MARKETING SYSTEM

THE STEP-BY-STEP, EASY-TO-IMPLEMENT,
"HOW-TO" GUIDE TO QUICKLY BUILD
A CONSISTENT MARKETING AND SALES
SYSTEM IN SINGAPORE

MICHAEL VECTRA TAN

System Blueprint: Ultimate Marketing System

The Step-by-Step, Easy-to-Implement, "How-to" Guide to Quickly Build a Consistent Marketing and Sales System in Singapore

Michael Vectra Tan

Printed by CreateSpace, An Amazon.com Company
Available from Amazon.com and on Kindle

This publication is written to provide accurate and authoritative information on the subject matter covered. The publisher does not provide legal, accounting or other professional services, and this publication is sold on this basis. If legal or other expert assistance is required, the services of a competent professional person should be sought.

ISBN: 9810939507
ISBN-13: 978-9810939502

DEDICATION

This book is dedicated to all entrepreneurs and business owners out there, striving to make the world a better place.

CONTENTS

HOW TO USE THIS BOOK

As stated in the title, this is a System Blueprint, and only someone who wants to build something reads a blueprint. So please join the complimentary Radiation Marketing Gold Membership (Worth $39.97, details in Part V), and finish up all the Action Guide (Indicated by the highlighted grey box below) that comes complimentary with this book, and start implementing all the ideas! The magic of knowledge is not in knowing, but in doing and applying what you know!

✳   # Action Time!   ✳

Now, if you are thinking, "How fast can I do this? Can I even do it at all?" Let me assure you that you can. It can all be done easily, as long as you have the desire to do it. Not every step has to be implemented and I have listed out the steps you should take in order of priority in the Gold Members Area, so not to worry, everything is covered!

If you are just starting out or need help in marketing your business, I absolutely recommend that you get my 90 minutes "Instant Business" consultation. You might have to spend a little, but with the personal coaching and consultation that I provide, you will be able to start your own business much, much faster and cheaper than it would have required.

If you own a ACRA Registered Business operating in Singapore, you may eligible for Government grants, reimbursable by SPRING Singapore, to help you generate a consistent flow of leads!

Either way, there is something for everyone, so do check out the complimentary **Gold Member's Area** to get started!
(See Part V of the book)

PS: Online social media and marketing can change at the snap of the fingers. Don't miss the online updates to this book in the Gold Member's Area!

PART I: OVERVIEW

Everyone is in sales. No, really.

When you are job hunting, you are selling yourself and your time in exchange for money. You can actually sell yourself better if you have your own website and videos demonstrating your expertise. This is why LinkedIn is so powerful, as it helps people to promote, "buy" and "sell" talents.

When you are proposing your ideas to higher management, or explaining your concepts so that your colleagues can follow, you are selling your ideas.

That's why I believe that even if you are not in sales, you will still benefit from reading this book by looking at the things in this world from a sales and marketing perspective, where everyone is thinking, "What's in it for me?".

Everything you need in sales and marketing stems from the M3 Triangle, consisting of Market, Message and Media. If it helps, you can also think of the triangle in terms of Economics, Conversion and Traffic, which is linked to Market, Message and Media respectively.

There has been many arguments against marketing, about how it creates waste and excess need, but it is absolutely necessary and is also the way our economy works, and improves itself. I do, however, also agree, that a powerful marketing system such as this, described in the pages of the book, if scaled up, can move and shape entire cultures and behaviors of the society. Obviously, this can negatively affect our society if it falls in bad hands. I am acting under the assumption that everybody reading this is an honorable and ethical person, selling products and services that will benefit their customers … if this isn't you, please return this book to the bookshelf and find something else to do. And this is more for your benefit than that of other people. There has been many times where I have seen people gain at the expense of others, but somehow this always gets back at them over time, leading to their eventual regret. History is rife with such examples as well, so it will do you well not to follow in their misguided paths.

CHAPTER 1:

MARKETING TRIANGLE

This first chapter is on the overarching concept of marketing, which can be explained using the Marketing Triangle. Every time you require directions on where your marketing should go, always come back to the marketing triangle as the basis on which you should build your marketing upon. As long as you stick closely to these principles, you will not go wrong, and your business will prosper.

MARKET

Are you a salesperson or consultant? Chapter 2 will help to correct your mindset, so that you can sell and market easily, in a way that your customers find helpful and appreciates. I'm sure this will help you find plenty of areas for improving your products and services as well.

In Chapter 3, the Pareto Principle is applied to sales and marketing so that you can create a system that provides maximal value for every customer.

Do you know what your ideal customers look like? What is their age? What do they like to eat or read? What are the pressing problems they want to solve right now?

Chapter 4 and 5 is about understanding your market in order to create your product. It also helps to structure it in a way that it is easy for people to try, trust and buy your products and services. If you get this right, you will get customers beating a path to your door step, and this is where you want to position yourself to be.

There are businesses out there who are actually losing money as they make more sales. That's ok if they have lots of cash to burn or if their main purpose is to drive out competitors. But I am pretty sure that most business owners' main reason for being in business is to make a profit. And that is what this book is geared towards - making money. Which is where the money math come in.

Don't worry, I am not talking about accounting and whether it should be on accrual or on cash basis, or if that is a credit or debit balance.

I am referring to simple revenue, expense and profit. This aspect consists of understanding your market, what they want and how much would they pay for a particular type of products and services.

You must know your own economics like the back of your hand, which will typically include your fixed costs in running your business, and each how much each customer can add to your total revenue, and how much of that will become profit.

The Essential Numbers will help you to focus on growing your business profitably, so that you know what's your limit and when to stop, allowing you to make money for every new customer you acquire. With this knowledge, we can then create your personalized marketing plan, which will form the foundation upon which you will build your unique marketing system.

The next part, Part III, breaks down and explains marketing messages that you should be conveying to your customers, and also how to make it irresistible and engaging.

MESSAGE

The purpose of your marketing message is for your customers to choose to respond and start a relationship with you or your business, so that you can market to them continually in a cheap and efficient manner. In order to do that, you must have a different, more useful and absolutely compelling message for your customers, rather than just another "I'm great, buy me!" message.

When your message becomes useful, it builds trust. And you need lots of trust from people before they will take the plunge and buy from you. They want to solve a problem and that's what you should be telling them more about. However, to build trust, it usually takes more than a single message, so your message must be compelling for them to request that you communicate with them more. As time goes on, and as you give them more useful information, they will want more stuff from you. This will cumulate to a point, where you can then offer your products and services and people will WANT to buy from you. You no longer have to sell to them. In Chapter 8, I cover how trust can be destroyed, as well as the many ways you can build trust.

Building trust is the easiest way to sell, otherwise you will not be spending the time effectively. For example, if you choose to convince others to WANT your product, there will be a lot more objections to overcome. Even when people WANTS to buy your product, there are significant hurdles to clear. Don't make things harder than it needs to be for yourself. The few rules of selling in Chapter 6 will help you to avoid making common mistakes and help you to become an esteemed and sought after consultant in your industry.

Next up are a few key platforms you will need to spread your message, and how to easily and effectively use them.

MEDIA

Media refers to the platform you will be using to communicate your message, to start getting people to trust and believe you. Spending more money means shouting louder to get heard, but whispering a highly attractive offer will get you heard too. This means if you have a good message, it only needs to be seen once or twice to be remembered. This allows a drastically smaller advertising budget. The idea here is that in today's competitive environment, every cent must be accounted for, and you don't have to spend unnecessary energy (read: Cash) shouting louder than you need to. The energy should be channeled elsewhere, like serving your customer better, or trying to provide them greater value.

Also, not all media platform are created equal. Even if you have a high-converting message, using direct mail drops or giving out flyers usually still costs more per Lead than Online Advertising, due to the connective power of the internet. Of course, online advertising has its drawbacks as well, so it depends on how you use it.

In Chapter 17 - The Unlimited Traffic Technique, I will explain how to cheaply and effectively test and improve your Message so that it will become profitable on any advertising platform you can think of! When you have positive advertising ROI on conventional media like radio and television advertisements, this is usually equates to a HUGE amount of leads. It is not easy to reach there, but when you do, be sure you have sufficient capacity or get ready to scale up!

In all businesses, the Marketing Triangle must always be at the core. Furthermore, most business owners fail to grasp that the "Market" must come first, followed by "Message" and the last will be "Media". But most business owners skip right to the "Media".

Business owners' are usually thinking "I need more customers...so, maybe I should take a newspaper ad...maybe I should re-do my website...maybe I should do direct fliers drop to every household."

Here's a golden nugget of wisdom: You must have the right target market who wants what you have to sell, and then your message must be laser focused and finely sculpted before you even BEGIN to consider the media you'll use to communicate it.

Why do so many businesses jump right to the "Media" part of the equation? Well, one main reason behind this traditional thinking and how marketing decisions is made is that business owners get "sold" on the media. Advertising agencies and media sellers are mainly concerned at how much profit *they* will make, and so their focus is selling you media that is profitable for them. Your results are of little, if any, concern to them.

They buy up different expensive media and put out similar messages, which doesn't stand out and probably not targeted at the right market. Needless to say, it fails miserably.

PART II: ECONOMICS

When you are in business for profit, there are a few important numbers you absolutely need to keep track of. It tells you if you are getting new leads, and if they are profitably converting into customers. In other words, you can actually predict your future income now, so that you can adjust the course of your business when it's still early.

As a business owner, always remember that bad economics will definitely kill your business, and no amount of marketing will be able to save it.

This Part also corresponds to the "Market" component of the Marketing Triangle.

CHAPTER 2:

THE CONSULTANT MINDSET

A consultant provides solutions that other people want to buy, giving information on the benefits the buyer will get. A salesman tries to get people to buy his product by providing information on how good the product is. The difference is in the way the product or service is communicated to other people. It should be seen as a solution to other people's problems, rather than a product which you want people to buy.

There is no way to properly build a working Marketing and Sales System without knowing this difference.

You need to know, not just believe, that you are selling something that works, and you should know how long it takes to work, what are its limitations and how to overcome the limitations. This will require you to have extensive knowledge of not only your products and services but also the reasons why your customers want to purchase the item for.

Sometimes people also have this self-limiting belief that just because they do not think the product or service is worth it's price, others will perceive it that way as well. Also, even if your prospect NEEDS certain products more urgently, doesn't mean they will WANT to buy the urgent products first.

"Why?", you ask. Well, because different people have different perceptions about the value of their time and the value of a purchase. And just because they need it, does not mean that they want it.

Alcoholics will give us a fine insight into this aspect of human psychology. They probably NEED help to quit drinking. But do you think they WANT to quit? And when they do want to quit, it's usually because of some other reason than the need to do it.

So you must always remember just because you think people need it, or even if they really do need your products and services, does not mean they want it. If they do not want it, they definitely will not take out their wallet to pay you.

You have to know what your customers are thinking about so that you know what your customers want before they even know themselves. Sometimes, your customers do not know what they want, and if you don't provide any recommendations, they just don't buy.

THE CONSULTANT SELF IMAGE

Now, take a long hard look at yourself. Do you have a powerful image of yourself in your own mind? Do you happily tell other people about what you do for a living? What about in more details?

If your answers to the above questions are negative, that means you have a poor self-image about your work and you will knowingly or unknowingly sabotage your own attempts to improve your selling. Here is another reason why you must question your own self-image: **How you define your self-image determines how much you can earn.**

The cliché, "You are only limited by yourself" could not have been more apt. Visualize and imagine the market as an ocean where you can remove money from. Whether you can use a spoon or a bucket to scoop the money from, the ocean does not care and you should not either. What you remove is very unlikely to cause any changes to what others can get out of the ocean, unless you are already a very significant player in the market.

Our free market system is not a zero sum game. When people pay you for your product and services, they are receiving more value than the cash amount they have paid for. Otherwise, you can be pretty sure that no one will pay you. So actually, the more money you remove from the ocean, the more value there is in the world.

Here are some raw material for your own self-image. A smart and hardworking sales professional in any field, whether insurance, real estate, automobiles, cleaning products or even multilevel marketing can build up an income in 10 years, that is equivalent to a doctor or lawyer who spent 10 years of paid studies and another 10 years of actual practice added together. How is it that possible?

Our society is a very intricate weaving of interdependence. The fireman who may save your life tomorrow is only able to do it because his own life was saved by a safety harness that was sold to the department by a sales representative. The prominent senior doctor was only able to operate on the patient with the help of sophisticated technology sold to the hospital by knowledgeable sales professionals in the medical product field. Not a single person, family, company or institution can survive long without the influence of countless sales professional. If every sales professional stayed home for 1 week, I believe the entire economy would grind to a halt, and society would be in chaos.

The skills and expertise of top sales professionals definitely rivals most other professionals in breadth if not in depth. This group of people are psychologists, confidants, consultants, product engineers, business advisors, family advisors all rolled into 1 and is definitely a powerful creative force to reckon with. They not only have comprehensive product knowledge, know their business well, but they also know their customers' and clients' business problems to provide them with solutions.

You, as a business owner and sales professional, must acknowledge that you have chosen a noble path by selling, and you are making a difference in many people's life! Make sure the 5 points below apply to you, if not, create situation so they apply!

1) A Healthy, Vibrant & Strong Self-Image

You must see yourself as a knowledgeable professional, providing real value to your clients. You are deserving of their trust and also of the rich rewards for your efforts. You do not fear losing a sale, because you know there are many, many others who needs and want to buy your product. You are not just selling for the commission, but rather, for the greater purpose of serving humankind.

2) Believing and Understanding Your Product

You must know what you offer is superior to other alternatives in important ways and that it provides good value for your clients and is praised by customers already benefitting from it. You know when it works, and when it does not work so that you can make the best recommendation, all for the benefit of the customers

3) Confidence In Yourself

This is the kind of confidence that comes from competence. You have good communication skills, a pleasant and effective personality with good listening skills. In other words, you know how to sell. And you have a solid, persuasive multi-part sales script, ready to adjust and adapt, unlike a canned presentation. You must be organized and straightforward in asking for an action at the end of every presentation, because you know you are providing exceptional value and that your customers need it.

4) Understanding Your Customer

You know your customers before they even know themselves when it comes to your products and services, because you know what is the norm and what are the outliers in the industry.

For example, tailors know how much is too baggy, and how little is too tight. Some more perceptive consumers may know, but most of us trust our tailors without a second thought. That is why we are there in the first place. We want the expertise of other people when it comes to buying a specialized item that we know we are not and do not want to be as proficient as the specialists.

You know your prospect's doubts and fears so that you can sooth and allay them before they even know it's presence. You should also know your prospects always have this temptation to avoid confrontation and decision, and hence you need to guide them towards the products and services that matches their wants and commitment level at that point in time.

For example, you can always offer a trial or cheaper version of your product so that your prospects can feel that they can purchase and receive exceptional value from regardless if they continue onwards with the actual product or not.

5) Honest Enthusiasm

Not the type that you try to project that is outside of your own personality, but genuine enthusiasm based on enjoying selling, meeting with people and solving clients' problems. People can sense and feel when you are genuine, and your enthusiasm can then be transferred to them so that they become excited about buying your products.

I've heard top salespersons say that selling can simply be viewed as a transfer of enthusiasm, and I agree. You need to have enthusiasm so that you can transfer it in the first place. And if you manage to do it well, you will not even need to sell. People will want to buy.

See, it is always about giving enough information about how your products and services *benefit* your prospects, so that they will feel, "Hey, this is great value!" and they will stand in line to buy your stuff.

You must also know that all negative influences and distractions will sap your motivation and enthusiasm for your work, and you must absolutely remove such distractions in your life.

If it seems like I'm asking you to change you're your friends, you might have to. You know best what kind of company your keep, and it is *very difficult* to keep your mind totally blocked off from the negative influences around you.

If you can't find any good company, do not fret. With the advent of technology, virtual companions essential for your success are at your fingertips. What I mean is you can find books, audio programs, podcasts, video training series, online seminars, etc by proven, successful people and constantly immerse yourself in them. And you probably do not even have to pay for it when you are just starting out, as there are many such videos available on Youtube. It's probably enough for around a year's worth of educational programme.

Whether you are commuting to and fro from work, or whether it is during the bit of spare time before your next sales appointment, listen to them, and have them keep you company. Yes, it does require some self-discipline to choose such educational contents over the latest game you want to play on your mobile phone, but this is what it takes if you really want to succeed.

It is my firm believe that many people know what they need to do to succeed, but the few who actually reach their goals are those who not only knows, but have the discipline to execute as well.

ENJOY SELLING

If the above 5 points apply, then you really ought to be enjoying selling. Because there are only 2 outcomes, if you are happy about your profession, show it and you will achieve exceptional results. In fact, set both big and small milestones where you celebrate your own success and achievements.

On the other hand, if you are not happy, then do something about it! There are only a few problems that you might have. Is it Skills Deficiency, Esteem Deficiency, Burn Out and Boredom or do you have an Integrity Conflict? Find out what it is, and get help on how you can deal with it. If you require external help, do sign up for my Platinum or Titanium Membership, and I'll walk you through the various steps to elicit the reasons why you are not performing as well as you should be!

USE MENTAL REHEARSAL

Boosting your Self Image by inspiring and motivating yourself is very important, because just by being confident, you will greatly change the way you carry yourself and present your solutions.

Let's take for example, you just received some bad news, and it is making you feel tired and disheartened. In this state, do you think that you can make a good sales presentation? Most likely not. But what if you took 5-10 minutes to visit your virtual Cinema and watch a rerun of your own success movie(s)? Imagine when you solved someone else's problems by providing them exactly what they needed, and did it so quickly that they didn't notice it! They then thanked you profusely, and could not have been more glad that they purchased from you. In fact, they are so happy that you got 3 new excellent referrals from them before the project was even finished.

You will definitely feel and perform much better than you would have compared to 10 minutes ago. But what actually changed? From an outsider's perspective, you merely went to sit down and closed your eyes for 10 minutes. However, there is a huge internal change in state, and also in the positive aura you would give off after that 10 minutes.

You must always have a fixed ritual for boosting your state so that you will definitely be on form, in the right state of mind, exuding the most positive aura possible before you enter any sales scenario. After all, you only have 1 shot to make a first impression. Better make it count.

A FEW OTHER POINTS

Objections Are Good

Only when you are selling high price products can you be at the high end of the income ladder. And you will definitely encounter plenty of problems and objections when you are selling a pricey software, simply because it is more complex. That's where you come in to clarify and simplify so that your prospective client can buy with a peace of mind. And make you some good money in the process.

Compare with a popcorn seller. Do you think they get lots of problems or objections? I think not, and that makes all the difference in salary level of these 2 salesperson.

Win Even When You Are Outclassed

Do you find that there are many situations where the underdogs, let's say in tennis, come out victorious? This is not by chance, but by hours or practice, of building up the self-image, of watching enough of your Success Movies in your Virtual Cinema. Eventually, what you think manifests itself in reality, but let's not get too spiritual here. If you have thought through a certain situation enough, you will already have the best solution on how to deal with it.

With this in your subconscious mind, the brain is able to quickly judge within split second the best way to return a certain type of serve, helping the player claim victory in the end. The same happens in business. With enough thought or visits to your Virtual Cinema, you naturally know which is the best way to deal with suppliers and customers in certain scenarios. This gives you the edge to choose the best business partners, and profit from your Virtual Cinema.

Using Affirmations

Again, this seems like a rather spiritual activity, but let's break it down. I believe in using affirmations for very specific activities, because I feel that it helps me more than using it in general.

Here are 2 examples.

> "I am smart and resourceful I will find a way to overcome this obstacle"
>
> vs
>
> "I will find someone who can help me to solve the problem"

I understand this is a rather simplified example, but I hope you can see the difference. The 1st statement will reinforce the fact that you have a problem that you need to solve, whereas the second statement will give you a more specific solution to the problem. Perhaps you can say that the 1st statement can lead you to the 2nd statement, which is fine as well, though it will take more time. The idea of using affirmations is that it requires you to think about what you want to get at a certain point in time, providing yourself with the clarity and focus on what you want. A majority of people really don't know what they want to do, aside from their dreams of being rich and travelling around the world. Dreams remain dreams unless action is taken to bring the dream closer to reality. Affirmations helps to clarify the actions you need to quickly take and anchor these actions in the mind as you remind yourself over and over again that you need to do this. As a result, it gets done earlier and better.

Your Conviction Against Their Resistance

This is all that there is in a sale. You need to have a strong enough believe in your product to overcome their resistance, though you have to take care not to be pushy in selling your product. In every sales interview, a sale occurs. Either you sell to your prospect that your product is valuable enough to overcome all the reasons why they should not buy, or the prospect sells you the reasons why he or she cannot or will not buy.

It is with genuine enthusiasm that you infect and convince others that they need your product, and make them buy from you, rather than making them feel being sold to. If the latter happens, their self-defense comes up and you will probably be shut off from the sale.

Control The Critic Within

Try not to be so critical of yourself all the time. Yes, you might have missed out on Points #3 and #6 in your presentation, but if you moved on the next point swiftly and confidently, nobody will notice a thing. Take a focused look at your objectives, if you have delivered a pretty good presentation, the audience enjoyed it, and you managed to get some clients (If that is your objective), then you did well!

Yes, you could have done better, but there isn't any need to beat yourself up. Just take note, don't never repeat the same mistake again. Everybody makes mistakes, but not everyone is able to stand tall in spite of their mistakes. But you are not "everyone", so stand tall and don't be so hard on yourself when you make a mistake. Learn, improve and grow.

SECRETS FOR AN ENJOYABLE SELLING EXPERIENCE

I have covered all the below in this chapter, so here's a quick summary!

Step 1: Use Your Imagination
Step 2: Strengthen your self-image
Step 3: Use Mental Rehearsal
Step 4: Use Affirmations
Step 5: Keeping your eye on the goal

We manufacture all the resistance that we encounter. Free your mind, and use your imagination. By now, I hope you have made the shift to a Consultant's Mindset, where you can now start an excellent career in selling, or take it to the next level if you have already started.

As again, when in doubt, get a coach. The right coach will save you lots of time and energy by showing you the quickest path to success.

Do not think that you only need to have this mindset when you are selling in person. You should also maintain this mindset even when you are creating systems for your business or creating your marketing materials. It would not be an exaggeration to say that this is a mindset that business owners and marketers should constantly keep at the forefront of their consciousness, if they would like to sell more and keep the business growing.

Also, I strongly believe throughout this process, you will be able to further tailor your product or service to fit in more closely with your customers. Hopefully, you are also able to improve the current version of whatever you are selling now, and bring your it to greater heights.

CHAPTER 3:

PARETO PRINCIPLE IN MARKETING AND SELLING

If you do not already know about the Pareto Principle, you should start familiarizing yourself with it. I would go as far as to say that it is a force of nature, much like gravity is.

Basically it says that 80% of the effects come from 20% of the causes. Like how:

- 80% of your sales comes from 20% of your best customers
- 80% of a company's sales come from 20% of its products
- 80% of a company's profits come from 20% of the time its staff spend
- 80% of a company's complaints come from 20% of its customers
- 80% of a company's sales are made by 20% of its sales staff

This book was also written with the 80/20 Principle in mind. Each of the chapters in this book can be expanded into a whole book by itself, in order to cover the 80% of the work that would account for an additional 20% of the results.

So take every point in every Chapter very seriously as it is all highly condensed, and every point can probably add a further 5% to your bottom line. If you have already done it, good for you, move on to another point. If you have already implemented most of the points in this book, do make a consultation appointment with me and I can show you which area will lead to your next breakthrough.

FRACTAL NATURE OF THE 80/20 PRINCIPLE

What does it mean?

Let us take this example of 80% of your sales coming from 20% of your best customers to explain this fractal nature.

This means for example, that this 80/20 principle applies to within the top 20% of your customers as well. So this means that within this top 20%, 80% of the sales will come from 20% of the customers. This means that the top 4% of all your customers contribute 64% of the sales! Now that you know this, remember that not all customers are born equal. Some wants your products much more than others, while many others only want the basic version.

When you are able to apply 80/20 over many layers, on one end you will be able to target the highest level customers who can and will buy anything you are able to offer, as long the right value is offered.

And on the other end, you can also craft products to suit lower level customers and appeal to the mass majority. This will allow you to create the most value for your market, and maximize your profit at the same time.

Now, note that this Principle is not absolute, in that it could be 60/30, 70/30 or maybe even 90/10. But know that it's always there - Even if you can't see it. Just like gravity.

There are a lot more applications of this 80/20 rule, which will be too wide in scope for this book to cover. Let me get down to just one thing we can actually use based on this rule.

Which will bring us to the Customer Ascension Ladder. Every customer will start out consuming free trials or information from you to start their relationship with your business. The more people you have starting out a relationship with you, even if it is for free stuff, the better. Because you can then start to nurture your relationship with them so that they start spending more and more with you in accordance with your Customer Ascension Ladder.

The Customer Ascension Ladder is based on implementing more price steps in your products and services, on both the higher end and the lower end as well. Everyone has a different perception of value and hence the dollar they are willing to spent on a particular group of product and service will differ. The very fact that they want some of your free stuff, shows that they will purchase some form of the products and services, if not from you, then from somebody else, perhaps at a different price point in a different version.

Finally, you should also offer some super high priced versions of the products and services you can offer. There are always those who are really into a certain hobby, and may spend upwards of 100 to even 1000 times of what the average customer spends. The below example demonstrates this point well.

An excellent example will be the coffee industry. Let's say you are offering free coffee samples to people, and 10,000 people tried the coffee sample.
Out of this 10,000 people, 8,000 will buy a cup of coffee for $1.
Then, roughly 1,600 people will buy a gourmet coffee for $4
320 people will buy premium gourmet coffee $16
64 people will join a coffee tasting workshop $64
12 will join a coffee seminar $256
2 people will buy a simple coffee machine for $1024
1 people will buy a premium coffee machine for $4096

Dollar Spend	$1.00	$4.00	$16.00	$64.00
No. of Customer	8,000	1,600	320	64

Dollar Spend	$256.00	$1,024.00	$4,096.00
No. of Customer	12	2	1

Fig 3.1: Every step of the dollar spending multiplies by 4
Every step of the customer number is 20% of the previous

While these are calculated figures, you should not be that far off from reality, if you follow this basic guide. If your numbers are large enough, you can even sell products at 4x of $4,096!

THE SALES FUNNEL

This is another angle you can use the Pareto Principle to look at selling and marketing.

At the top of the funnel, the mouth is much wider, because there are a lot of people who shows initial interest in the product, ranging from people who just curious and wanted to learn something new to warm prospects who need your products in the near future to red hot prospects who wants your product NOW.

Most business owners have no problem handling the red hot prospects, because they fit in to the majority of the sales process in many businesses: Salesperson call up prospect, delivers a sales presentation and after confirming the details, the sale is made.

However, a huge opportunity lies in the curious and the warm prospects, which if developed properly, can lead to an additional 2 to 3 times more customers than that which you are currently handling now.

A proper funnel will allow prospects to enter your Marketing Machine at absolutely any point in the sales process. It should also allow you to follow up cheaply and effectively, so that you have a continuously flow of prospects maturing at their own pace. When the time comes for them to buy, you will become the only clear choice.

As you follow through the Action Guides in this book, you will naturally be building your own customized Ultimate Marketing System!

---

* **Action Time!**
Complete your worksheet on **Customer Ascension Ladder** to help you brainstorm and create more versions of your products and services to maximize your Total and Average Customer Value!
~

CHAPTER 4:

THE 9 ESSENTIAL NUMBERS

Many people say that a business is all about numbers, and they are definitely right. But we all know that accountants can make unprofitable companies seem profitable and some big companies are frequently restating profits so what are the numbers that really make a difference?

The yearly accounts done by your accountant for meeting the Tax and Regulatory requirements are historic numbers and will tell you that your business is *dead*, long after you already folded. But I'm sure you would much rather know when your business is *sick*, and not when it is too late. What you want are numbers that you can work with on a month to month basis that tells you if your business is growing strong or has fallen ill, so that you have plenty of time to perform life saving measures for the business. Below are the 9 sets of Essential Numbers that all successful business owners have at their fingertips.

1) CPL (COST PER LEAD)

This is the amount spent for the customer to raise his hand and start the path down the funnel.

If you do a direct flyer drop of a 20,000 piece campaign, which should cost around SGD 900, and you received 20 leads before the deadline, usually set for 1 month from date of distribution, then your cost per lead is $40. Depending on a number that I explain later in this chapter, it could be winner or a total lossmaker.

The way to calculate CPL is the same even if you use other platforms such as TV, Radio, Newspaper, Google Adwords or Facebook.
Hence, you will actually have one CPL for each type of media and message that you use. This means you print message 1 on media 1, you will get CPL 1. If you use message 2 on media 1, this will give you CPL 2. So just having 2 different messages on 2 media will give you 4 different CPLs.

However, the trick here is to maximize your conversion ratio, which will minimize your CPL, on the cheapest medium first. Currently, the best medium is Facebook, which I will explain later. So you should use Facebook to test, trial and develop a killer message which converts at the highest rate, so that you can be profitable on even more expensive media which other companies cannot use.

Here's the scenario that would decide if you have a profit or loss making campaign: Let's say you know that 2 leads will give you 1 customer which will give you an average profit of $450 each.
So if it costs you $900 on direct flyer drop to reach the 20,000 people to generate 6 leads, you will break even immediately, and likely make a small profit in the near future as the other leads mature.
Let's say your marketing conversion now improved by 100%, and you now have 12 leads which gives you 6 customers, you will have a sustainable campaign which you want to run for as long as you can and scale up as much as possible. That is, of course, provided the numbers remain the same.

Now, let's say you are planning to use a more aggressive media, TV advertising to reach 100,000 people at $3000, but where you know the conversion rate is much lower. You will need 7 customers to break even based on the same situation, so you will need 14 leads to break even. Because you already tested you message cheaply on the earlier platform, you are now confident to spend the $3,000 to get your 14 leads.
If you had not refined your message, and it yielded only 10 leads, you would have made a loss on that medium, and missed out on that

group of customer that you can reach.

Note here that we are only calculating the immediate ROI.
There is also build up of brand equity in your Future Bank along the way. Not to mention you can nurture the rest of the other leads who might buy later or at a lower price or a different version of your product. Hence, basing the success or failure of an advertisement on the immediate ROI is a conservative number that is unlikely to go wrong.

2) CPS (COST PER SALE)

This is an important number to keep track of in order to manage your sales and marketing effort, because it aggregates all the important numbers and combine them into one.
This number includes all the costs of putting the prospect on the path including the cost of conversion (Salesperson's time spent, additional services and/or premiums given) into a customer, client and patient and it varies by source, method and effectiveness of the path.
For example, propects with the lowest CPL might end up to have the highest CPS, due to the additional steps required to convince and convert them into paying customers.
At the end of the day, you need to know your ATV, CV and LCV to determine the Maximum CPS (Max-CPS) you can have so that you are making money for every customer you take.

3) ATV (AVERAGE TRANSACTION VALUE)

The reason why upsells are so powerful is that increasing topline or revenue by only 10% will boost your Net Profit by a higher percentage, maybe like 25%. You should always be on the look out for ways where you can systematically increase the average transaction value.

Here's an example: You sell finger food at $3 per pack. You have already spent what you needed to to rent the place, get the customers here to buy your food. Of that $3, probably $2 went to the rent, advertisement and other variable costs and so you only made $1 per pack. If you managed to sell another drink at $1 to go along, taking away the variable cost (let's say $0.50) of providing the drink, you made another $0.50, which is a 50% increase in net profit, although you only increased your revenue by 33%. This is a simple example, but you should get the point. Not offering upsells simply leaves money on the table. It is within reach, but that you are simply too lazy to stretch a little to take it.

4) CV (CUSTOMER VALUE)

Things come in different shapes and sizes and your customers are the same. You should start dividing into and keeping track of the different A, B and C group of customers to find out their characteristics. This helps you to target your messages to find more Group A customers and reduce the number of Group C customers coming to you. You might even decide that your C customers are actually costing you money to keep, and so you can decide to fire them altogether, if it's possible.

For example, if some customers use too much customer service time, they may not be the right fit for your company, and it might be more beneficial for them to do business with other types of business structure, for example where more face to face interaction is part of the company culture.

5) CTP (CONTRIBUTION TO PROFIT)

After you breakdown your customers into different segments, you can then tell which groups are more profitable, by measuring their average contribution to profit. As again, those customers who require more care will reduce your bottom line by increasing the amount of servicing costs.

This figure also lets you see if you should take additional customers, even if it is at a reduced price. Sometimes, your overheads can be eating you alive, and some income is better than no income at all. Note that it should at least cover the variable costs required to provide the product, and it should not greatly cannibalise normal sales.

6) LCV (LIFETIME CUSTOMER VALUE)

This number gives you the total value of the customer, and it contains FA (Future Account) value. It is actually a combination of CV, CTP and the length where you manage to keep customers active.

This number gives you a good gauge of how much you add into your FA once you acquire a new customer or re-activate a lost one. This also helps to keep the cost of losing every single customer in sight so you can determine how much to spend to keep them active.

By now, you should have noticed that all of these numbers are interlinked, and you will need a combination of these numbers to make informed business decisions.

For example, you feel that your flyer drop campaign is working out well, and you are now considering between another round of flyer drop or advertisement on a magazine. All you have to do is to ask yourself the below 2 questions to decide which form of advertisement will maximize your profit.

1) What is the actual or estimated CPL, CPS and LCV of the customers from each of the advertisement?
2) How do the above values compare with the CPL, CPS and LCV of customers from alternative media available to you?

This is a start, and you can definitely delve deeper, depending on whether it is worth your time to drill down, but without these basic numbers, you would not know if you should maintain, scale up, scale down or perhaps even utilise all media if your numbers are good!

7) PA STATISTICS (PRESENT ACCOUNT)

This number is represented by the actual cash amount that you have now, which also includes the income you will earn in the current day or month.

By this, I mean the actual cash amount that you can remove from your business. Sometimes this number seems lower than it actually is, because you forgot to take into account the business trip you took which felt more like a vacation, or a car that you actually do not require and things like that. Take a hard look at your business and determine what is the actual profit you have made so you can manage your Present Account better.

PA statistics include the numbers of customers that purchased today and their actual ATV, as this will immediately affect the amount of money that will be deposited later in the night.

Your PA should be constantly growing, as you take money out of your business to "pay yourself first". Unless you deliberately and consciously treat your business as a hobby, your business is really only there so that you can generate value for others so that you as the business owner can remove cash from.

8) FA STATISTICS (FUTURE ACCOUNT)

This actual equity you have in your business. Now equity is a tricky word, because assets and inventory which are normally overstated in the balance sheets are included as equity as well. What it is really worth, is the amount you can actually sell them for, and not the depreciated purchase value. Business owners con themselves into believing the business is more than it is worth because of all these figures.

To take a hard look at assets (Plant, Machinery and Inventory), based on the price they can currently be sold for, this number is usually much lesser than the historic value, which is frequently used as the base to measure equity.

However, there is one asset that business owners frequently undervalue or do not measure at all. This asset also has real calculable value and it is the relationship the business have with its list of customers.

Assuiming that a restaurant has a 1,000 people on its birthday list, and based on a historic ratio of 75% turn-up rate (upon sending them a birthday voucher) and ATV of $40, we can easily measure the FA value of the customer list to be $30,000 per year. And this does not include their ocassional visits to the restaurant.

This is real equity that you can use to calculate the value of your business when you would like to sell it off in the future.

FA statistics might include the number of customers who join the birthday program, mailing list, rewards programme, incoming leads in the trial programme or any other follow up strategy that consistently and measurably generate profits in the future. Every business can and must find a way to manage this FA statistic, because it is equally, if not more important than the PA numbers, because it will tell you how the business will perform in the next quarter or even year with the right numbers.

The relationship do deteriorate over time, by around 10% every month every month where no follow up is done. That is why not following up is the same as flushing money down the toilet bowl. Absolute wastage. See more about follow-up in Chapter 7.

9) SE (SALES EFFECTIVENESS)

This is the efficiency of each subfunction of every individual parts of the business such as the **percentage of**:

1) Customers calling in and converted to kept appointments
2) Website visitors who gave full or partial contact information
3) Walk in customer where contact information was collected
4) Walk in customer who buy
5) ATV of current against other similar stores

The action guide for this chapter is combined with that in the next chapter, in the Radiation Marketing Action Plan.

CHAPTER 5:

5 PILLARS OF MARKETING

You only need to have something to sell to have a business.

However, you need to know **HOW** to sell it well to have a successful business. If you think hard about it, you will realize that the money is really not in how well your product or service perform, but rather in how well you *communicate* your product or service will perform.

In truth, your prospect won't know if what you are selling is truly superior to what others are selling right? Unless they buy it and try it, of which your customer knows it will be too late to turn back. Hence, do not rely on product superiority as an entitlement to the fact that it will sell well. Because it will not. It will only sound like you are tooting your own horn when you keep emphasizing the features your products have.

The 9 Essential Numbers for your business is the first Pillar, which we have covered in the previous chapter. It will help to keep you focused and motivated by reminding you of the profit potential of your business, and it will also guide you to make profitable choices among the many marketing methods and media around.

Your essential numbers tells you early what your business's profit potential is like. Then you can decide if it excites you, because if it does not, you still have time to either create additional services to increase your margins, or you can pull the plug early before you incur heavy losses. These numbers will also keep you conscious of how much you can spend to acquire a new customer profitably, so that you are always making a profit.

YOUR UNIQUE SELLING PROPOSITION(USP)

I have heard that one good way to determine if you have a strong USP is to see if other business can use your USP. If they can, then it is probably too generic. As it states, it must be unique, for example in offering a watertight guarantee for your customers, with a record breaking timeframe and a truly different product or service experience. Or it could be a unique company culture or policy that other companies cannot claim that they have.

Perhaps it can also be an industry norm that your company bends or breaks. Or a special story that you can use to tell your customer. Or a common enemy that both you and your customers share, which will make your customers associate with you.

Only companies geared towards offering a special offering can use a specific USP, although ALL businesses can have a USP truly unique to their own business. It really just requires some effort to think through how you can package your products and services so that you can create and use a certain USP.

You must elicit these specific points that are unique and can't be generically applied to other companies and incorporate them into a compelling message that makes people instantly want to find out more about. This will make your message truly stand out and capture people's attention. This is the message you should be using as your USP.

KNOWING & "HIRING" YOUR IDEAL CUSTOMER

What do I mean by knowing your ideal customer? You must know, or at least make an intelligent guess about the characteristics and qualities that your ideal customers have. Here are some pointers, which you will also find in the Marketing Action Plan:

Who qualifies?	How much money do they make?
Where do they live?	What makes them qualify?
Do they drive?	What age group are they in?
Are they male or female?	What stage of life are they in?
Do they have children?	Are they in a specific industry?

How old are their children?	What's their job title?

Knowing a few, or better yet, all of the above aspects about your ideal customers will help you create a message so specific that your customers will feel compelled to look further and request for more information just because it is talking specifically about them, even when they might not be interested in your product or services at this point in time.

Here is a more advanced concept of specific targeting, which I will show you how to do it later using Google and Facebook in Chapter 14 and 15. It works like this:

Let's say you want to sell a book on productivity. Let's say you looked a little further and realized they also like, Edge of Tomorrow, a movie with a time loop concept.

You can then target them specifically by adding this statement as a headline, "Wish you had more time to perfect your craft like Tom Cruise in Edge of Tomorrow?" This will easily add 50% to 100% to the response from your advertisements!

And by "hiring", I am actually borrowing the concept of hiring employees. Business owners usually hire employees, by stating the specific skill sets and characteristics that they want in their potential employees, and getting new customers is very similar in this respect.

First up, you have to know the characteristics of your best customer, someone who will derive great value from what you have to offer. Then put the characteristics in words and incorporate it in your marketing message. When they see you are referring specifically to them, you will capture their attention and they will naturally want to know more information and promotions from you.

LEAD GENERATION CORES

Once you have identified your ideal customer group, you will then need to create trust by showing that you have the solution that they want, by giving out your lead generation cores in exchange for their contact information.

These are the cheap and low threshold reports, eBooks or free/heavily discounted trials that you can create and give out to customers who request it from you. The main idea is to get customer's contact information so that you can follow up cheaply, or perhaps even for free. (See more about following up in Chapter 7) To achieve this, you only need to create tempting freebies by designing a good cover, logo or any suitable appealing design for your freebie. With the advent of Fiverr.com, anyone can purchase good designs at affordable price ($5 USD plus any add-ons that you might require).

Always remember that the fear of loss is greater than the desire for gain. This means that if your customers have even the slightest doubt about the quality or value of your product, then you can be sure that your advertisement will fail miserably. And that is the reason why you will need to start with a low threat-threshold product or service. It should be offering tons of value at a low price, or maybe even for free, so that your prospective customers can *try* to start trusting you. Because even if it is free, they still have to give you their time, so there really isn't anything that is truly free.

So if these Cores that you give out truly provides great value to customers, then they can start to trust you as a result of these positioning assets. However, if these positioning assets are of low or no value to prospective customers, they will become averse to any products you offer on the future. In these situations, even if you do get their contact details, the efficacy of your follow up marketing will already be greatly reduced. Hence, always ensure your lead generation cores are of good quality.

Good lead generation cores are always created with the concept of building trust by solving your potential customers problems first. Once people receive value from this, they will mature to become full paying customers over time.

MEDIA

What media should you be using then? This would have to depend on the scale and type of business you are in. Generally in this internet age, advertising via online platforms are a lot cheaper as compared offline platforms such as flyer drop, television or radio advertising. However, as I elaborate further in the unlimited traffic technique, the best source of traffic is a profitable source of traffic. Any traffic that can be used to convert prospects into paying customers profitably should be utilized, provided you have sufficient scale and capacity to provide your products and services to the increased surge in customers.

And since only when you are able to measure the ROI on your marketing dollars can you be sure whether the advertisement is profitable or not, you have to ensure that all advertisements are tracked and measurable.

Business owners might think that this kind of tracking is too much work and unnecessary, and they might be right. But usually, with single platform advertising, tracking is usually not that onerous, but merely requires the decision to put some thought into creating a tracking system that will work.

If you are doing complex multi-platform advertising, you probably have quite a sizable budget, and the ROI on tracking advertising messages is very likely be worthwhile. With the advent of so many affordable IT cloud services, tracking has never been easier. It does take time for one to get acquainted with the different services that you can integrate with your marketing campaign, so this is where I would suggest professional help should be sought to best optimize usage of your time. Common platforms that can help you to track results are Google Analytics, Facebook Ads Manager, mail auto-responder systems, and even event sign up platforms such as Eventbrite. These platforms are also especially effective once they are integrated together.

TAKE ACTION!

This is a rather short chapter, because there really isn't much point in telling you too much about irrelevant businesses.

A much better use of your time would be to roll up your sleeves and get started on the Marketing Action Plan to create a customized implementation plan to suit your current unique business situation.

Also, this plan is very likely to change from the time you first crafted it, to the time you actually implement it. Hence, get it done quickly and find a way to test your plan cheaply. For example, a moderate price product that you expect to sell well actually sells more poorly than your higher end product. This indicates that you have to adjust production capacity for your higher end product, or if that is not possible, to further increase the price of the higher end product.

There are yet many other possibilities, but you never know how or what to adjust until you put the plan into action.

---

* ## Action Time!

Complete the **Radiation Marketing Action Plan, which include The Essential Numbers** to create a crystal clear version of your marketing and advertising strategy to quickly and effectively grow your business! ~

PART III: CONVERSION

This Part corresponds to the "Message" component of the Marketing Triangle.

RESPONSE ADVERTISING VS BRAND ADVERTISING

Your message to your customers are conveyed by your advertisement messages, which can be divided into 2 main types.

The first type is Brand advertising, which requires a huge budget to get your brand recognized. However, even if the market recognizes your brand, they may not buy your products and services, so when many small business owners tried to do this, they find that advertising "does not work".

Media Executives are often told, "It's not about selling, it's about image building and building up the brand", going by the theory that once recognized, consumers will automatically buy from you. In the past, you might create a lot of excitement with your Brand as a result of brand building ads, because you might be *the only* bakery, nail salon or clothing store in the area. This is very unlikely to be the case now.

The other type is Response advertising, which requires interested customers to respond to whatever you have to offer. This is more suitable for any business if you wish to have a leaner advertising budget, and this is the method I always advocate in my Radiation Marketing Systems.

Here are a few key points to remember when crafting your marketing message.

1)   The purpose of your message is to make you money

When designing your marketing message, always keep this point in mind. You can spend a ton on buying awareness, familiarity and recognition, but this is no assurance that you will receive value or power from the marketplace. It might even lead you to bankruptcy. So make sure that every dollar you put out there bring some of their friends back. If not, refine and resume.

2)   Keeping your ideal customers in mind

To maximize your marketing dollars, it is pertinent to have a laser focus on a very specific audience who are inclined to buy from you. You should then develop an "ideal customer" characteristics such as their age, gender, income, interests and geographic location. This will give you a good idea on how to craft a personalized message to reach your customer avatar. You should also try to find out what magazines, websites or radio stations they frequent, as this knowledge will help you to decide which media will reach the best customers at the lowest cost. This will be covered in Part III of this book.

3)   Apply response marketing to your ads

There are a few rules to adhere to as you are starting out on your direct marketing journey, which I shall cover in the Chapter 7. You will need to calculate a measurable return on your marketing dollars so that you can decide whether it will be profitable or not. This way, you can choose to improve the advertisement response rate or scrap the campaign altogether and try a totally different approach. You will still be building your brand, but your initial sales, designed to be smaller, ideally should cover your marketing costs, so you can build your brand for free!

4)   Benefits, not Features!

Too many people forget that to sell something, it must be all about what the customer will get. Not how good you are. For example, if you want to buy a mousetrap, would you want

1) A mousetrap that is NASA designed, with Space Age metal for maximal durability and efficiency OR
2) A mousetrap which guarantees you a mouse free home in 2 days, with a double money back guarantee?

If you have a bad enough mouse infestation, I'm betting you would go for choice 2. All because it gives you the benefits that you are looking for. As humans, we are forever in the "WIIFM" (What's in it for me?) mindset. Always remember this, and your marketing messages will spread by themselves.

This is a point worth repeating again: Remember to state the user benefits, and not the product features.

5)   It's not your products or your copy; It's the offer!

Here's a fact for you to digest: Anything can be sold, and sold well. Yes, this includes crap that is actually not useful to people, including scams. The reason why so many people still fall for these is because they are sold well, and to sell well you will need a great offer.

A good offer will focus on people's wants, the circumstances under which they want it, at the price they want it. Everyone has a different price level for the same product and service, so you will have to find the magic number that enough people wants and still makes you a good profit. If not, you will have to add enough benefits to your product to increase the value that people can gain from your product.

TO BRAND OR NOT TO BRAND

You must take care to note that I am not saying that branding is not important. My brand, Radiation Marketing is worth a lot to me because it distinguishes me from the market.

What I AM saying is, branding can and should be done without direct investment. Branding should come as a positive side effect of offering good products and services at a great value. It can be tempting to copy the advertising and marketing strategies of big companies, especially if they are backed by high-profile, high-priced agencies. However, to ensure maximum profit with a powerful brand

and a positive relationship with a loyal group of customers that remain excited about doing business with you, then put your energy and marketing dollars into direct response marketing that makes you money while simultaneously building a valuable and powerful brand as a free by-product.

Your brand should help your customers to cut through the clutter and chaos in the marketplace. A brand that makes you the undisputed choice for customers to choose from over your competitor. A brand that tells consumers what to expect and what not to expect.

Make your brand about persuading your customers to engage and act.

CHAPTER 6:

6 COMMANDMENTS OF SELLING

If you want to sell easily and effectively, below are a few steps that you absolutely should follow. There are situations where the below rules might not applicable, but I would say they are far and few in between. More likely, you have not given it sufficient thought, or tried enough methods to work within the rules. It might be elusive, but once you find it, the system will do the work for you.

1) **No cold calling ever**

   Even if they do set up appointments to meet up with you, how many of them actually buy? Imagine the amount of resistance you will have to overcome. If cold calling is already working for you, great! You can further make your selling even more efficient by restructuring that information into a medium like video or a book, and let the medium generate leads and pre-sell on your behalf.

2) **Generate leads with problem solving information**

   People buy things to solve their problem, and they probably want to solve their problem now. Give them the information they need to decide that you can solve their problem for them. Don't focus on yourself, focus on them: your customers. For example, if you are selling beauty products, don't say how organic your products are, say how safe it is for them to use it.

3) **Super charge your credibility by authoring, speaking and publishing quality information**

Many times, consumers do not buy even if they want a certain product or service. The reason is because they simply do not trust the shop enough to start a business transaction. The best way to overcome this is to start creating marketing materials that are worth paying for. High quality, well organized, information. This way, people look up to your brand as the industry leader in your field. This automatically decreases price resistance while increasing trust, all at the same time.

4) **Find out how much you are willing to pay for a new customer**

Sometimes, companies spend more than what's it's worth for a new customer. This is fine if it is a recognized fact, and done in a controlled manner. However, some companies are just not aware of their numbers and end up over spending. This is a surefire way to bleed their bank dry, so be aware.

5) **Keep contact with your customers, as they are all valuable assets who are much more inclined to buy from you**

One great sin a lot of companies commit is that they do not do proper follow up. Most don't do it because they do not want to 'spam' their customer. But who said it has to be done that way? Your follow up communication can be as interesting and informative as you design it to be. It can be true however, that poorly designed follow up filled with pure company centric messages like sales and promotion messages will tell your customers that you are more interested in yourself than them. Obviously, you will lose customers' trust and respect this way, and better follow up messages should be devised.

6) **Find prospects who are looking for you, as they are much likelier to buy from you**

It is an incredibly tough sale to make to customers if they are not looking for you or not inclined to buy from you. It can be done, but it will probably take you twice as much effort in twice as much time as you would normally need. Hence, marketing systems should be designed to qualify and disqualify customers at the same time and only bring prospects who are looking for your type of products and services to the sales team, while keeping the lookers in another follow up system until they are ready to buy.

"ARE YOU TELLING OR SELLING?"

You've probably heard the saying and that the key to sales success is to be a good listener more than a good talker. Both of these points are true BUT it misses this key distinction: You need to ask the right questions in order to elicit the responses from your prospect, so that you have the right information to close the sale.

Telling is just saying something that may or may not have any effect on the other party. Selling is saying something in a persuasive manner so that it causes the other party to act. To be really persuasive, you have to know what the other party wants, and that's where asking the right question is extremely important. It will tell you the underlying psychological reasons behind what your prospects want so that you can adjust the sales presentation, even if what you're offering is really the same. Doing this this will greatly boost your closing rate and bank balance.

Here are the three simple, but really powerful and specific questions that will help you to uncover your prospect's buying criteria.

1)   What are you looking for or what is most important to you in <<Your product or service here>>?

You can also further expand on this point by asking, "What are the three crucial things you absolutely need in a _____?"
These 2 questions immediately determines the reasons why someone is thinking about buying a product or service like the one you're offering. These are your prospect's hot buttons and also the benefits he is looking for.
As sales people, we tend to talk about each and every benefit of our product or service. But really, a benefit is only a benefit if the customer says it is.
Here is an advanced and much forgotten sales point: The only benefits you should be talking about are the ones your prospect has specifically told you they want.
Okay, now read that again.

You might kill a sale by boring a prospect when you start talking about benefits that don't interest him.

This first question tells you what to focus on, so you do not make this mistake.

2) What is important about that?

You want your prospect to think deep and give you the reason why the benefit(s) he wanted are actually what he wants. In essence, he is telling you how to sell to him. Sometimes, people initially comes up with a superficial reason why they want something, but turns out this is not the actual reason, causing you to fail the sale. You want the REAL reason why they want your product in order to make a successful sale.

3) To make sure I clearly understand, ultimately what would that <<Prospect's Answer to Question 2>> do for you?

Powerful stuff. You are taking your prospect on a deeper psychological discovery process where she will tell you the real reasons, the subconscious reasons, why she wants to buy a product or service like the one you are offering.

It might seem weird when I put it like this, but really, most people do not know what they want. And that's the purpose of these questions: To elicit the prospects real and immediate needs.

Now that you have these 3 questions, using the points that I have covered in the Consultant's Mindset, think of the various ways you can angle your product so that they are more likely to accept it.

I know your product can solve multiple problem that different customers might have, but you only need to explain how you can solve that 1 or 2 main problem that your prospect might have for them to buy from you. There is no need to explain everything, and doing so only wastes your precious time and might bore and confuse the prospect as well.

Remember to paraphrase and repeat the exact same words that your prospect uses. Every word has at least a slightly different meaning and you want those precise words that trigger the specific and positive feelings your prospect has.

Also, run through these points with your customer avatar, and think of what are the things they want and what objections you might face. Never forget the Underutilized Power of Negative Preparations (later in this Chapter).

---

*   # Action Time!
Revise using the **Power Questions Action Guide,** to understand your customers at the psychological level and not merely sell them what they say they want, but to their inner desires to quickly and effectively grow your business!   ~

CAPTURING ATTENTION

In the movie "The Guilt Trip", inventor of an organic cleaner, Seth Rogen's character, Andy, was trying to sell his chemical cleaner based on the scientific facts of the product, which is pretty boring. He focused on what HE thought was interesting instead of what his audience would find interesting, and this did nothing to emotionally hook his audience.
Many business owners also make the same mistake of focusing on the features of the products, and not what the audience will want to know – the benefits, or the benefits of the benefit of the product.

The movie had a good ending, where the character Andy managed to capture the attention of a major sales network, by drinking his organic cleaner to show how safe the product is.

This obviously captures people's attention, by showing a benefit that it is very safe, to the point where you can drink it, and the benefit of this benefit is that customers will know that their family will be safe when they use this cleaner.

You will know that you are failing in this aspect when you see your prospect...
Shuffling in their seat

Checking their phone for emails

Staring at someplace other than you

Not engaged with you or asking questions

…then it's time to change your selling angle and try another one which will capture your customer's attention. Go back to using the Power Questions to elicit your prospect's hot buttons, and then do or say something that is as dramatic as drinking cleaning solution to capture your customer's attention from that angle.

No one, and I mean no one, will care about your product until you can identify a way to capture 100 percent of your audience's attention. In fact, this is the explanation behind why certain entrepreneurs get clients to buy and believe while others are often forgotten and ignored. And best of all, it's simple to do, once you understand it. When you can achieve this, you will no longer need to convince someone your product or service is cool or interesting or superior; your customers are much more inclined to believe what you say and trust your opinion.

THE UNDERUTILIZED POWER OF NEGATIVE PREPARATION

This point is linked to understanding your prospect as well. Different customers have different concerns for the same product, which is difficult to predict and answer satisfactorily when it suddenly surfaces.

Your best solution: Don't try to predict your prospect's concerns, instead, be prepared for EVERY possible situation where a concern might be raised, and shoot down the concerns in advance, before the question is even asked. Don't try to hide the problems, find creative methods to present them in a positive light. It is the best way to convince the other party, and also creates strong reputation for yourself in the marketplace and industry.

This works for all transactions, small and large, and is your best bet, especially in big ticket items like selling off a troubled arm of your business. The only thing is that you will need to justify your time taken for the Negative Preparation. The bigger the transaction value, the more time you should take to position the negative aspects of your product or services.

It takes time and effort to think through and prepare for all the objections that might arise during the presentation, and as again, this is the reason why so many people do not do this – They simply want to take the easy way out.
You might have realize that this is one of the key issue in many of the problems I have highlighted in this book, and hence I have dedicated the entire Part V of the book to address the time and self-discipline issues that many entrepreneur further improve upon.

7 PSYCHOLOGICAL TRIGGERS

In this last section of this chapter, let me talk about what some people call "Mind Control" techniques, and to a certain extent, they're right. You will be triggering the emotional responses in the mind of the prospect, so that what they do will be out of emotion, rather than by logic, which incidentally is the way people make buying decisions. They decide that they want it, then create reasons to justify and rationalize taking out their wallet to pay. Using these triggers is based on "Entering the conversation that is already in their mind". You do need to know what it is though, by giving it sufficient thought, before you can use these triggers effectively.

However to use this kind of techniques will require you to take a slightly more extreme position. It is likely that you are uncomfortable with using these techniques, however it is necessary if you wish to achieve maximal sales by using the most powerful method available in selling.
Now, do not feel ignoble in using these "Mind Control" techniques if you are selling a truly superior product that will benefit your customer, who will willingly buy from you again after experiencing your first product. However, if you know or feel that you are cheating your customers, know that the market will always come back for you. I strongly advise against this, as it is through our service to the market, that it rewards us. Short-term gains at the cost of long term equity like your brand is never going to go on to make you big

money. Even if it does, it will not last, so don't waste your time. Instead, build a superior product, and sell it with a peace of mind.

1) Shame

The ambition to escape the unwanted is present in more people, than for example, positive motivation, and hence easier to stimulate than the ambition for gain or benefit. Here's the Shame List, containing some key words that you can and should use to generate this kind of feeling:

The Shame List			
Foolish	Unwanted	Incompetent	Left out, left behind
Stupid	Pitied	Weak, Impotent	Looked down upon
Un-cool	Embarrassed	Gossiped about	Attached to a loser/ losing argument
		Cars, Home, Job	"living in loser town"

2) Emotional Pain

You can also use or write powerful sales presentation to inflict emotional pain. Usually the knife is already there, all you need to do is to find it and twist the knife a little more.

The Pain Generators
1: "All too familiar" situations
2: Personal confessions the reader identifies with
3: Reminders of suppressed negative feelings of self
4: Negative imagination triggered of others' poor perceptions of or disappointments with them.

3) Anger, Rage, Resentment

Everyone is angry about something and resents somebody. They feel they have been shortchanged in some or all aspects of life. You only have to find the source, remind people and bring it from a simmer to a boil. Then align your sales message with your prospective and now angered customers who will now feel a lot more inclined to do business with you: Because you understand their innermost feelings best.

The Anger Sources		
Immigration issues	The incompetent boss/colleague	Rich-gets-richer concept
Relationship issues	"Poor me" Concept	Political alignment

4) Mysticism

People like to, want to and choose to believe in SECRETS, conspiracies and even 'mystics' with mysterious, superior or unique power. They also frequently look (secretly) to this as the answer to why they aren't living life as they'd hoped. They believe this information is withheld from them and that once they got this new "shiny object" they will be able to achieve the life that they want. You can also think of it as a much more palatable way for people to accept it when things are not going their way.

"It's not my fault, people are conspiring against me, and there's nothing I can do."

Like how they can never lose weight, get rich or have great relationships, but the common factor is only themselves. Therefore, they can be made to look into the 'spiritual' for solution, cures and opportunities, if the conditions are right. The Mystical Array will help you to invoke these feelings, and give them a reason to believe you.

The Mystical Array				
Secrets	Conspiracies	Mysterious	Unique	Occult
Hidden	Obscure	Cryptic	Puzzling	Magic

5) Revenge, Vindication, Redemption

These are powerful feelings you can generate in your buyer, pushing their buttons enough to be bothered but not pissed, saying, "Well, how do you like me NOW?!"

The Dissed List		
Put down	Under-Estimated	Doubted, skeptical about
Disrespected	'Second class citizen"	Looked down on
Excluded	Not taken seriously, ridiculed	"Such things are not for you"

6) Fear and Insecurity

Humans are driven more by fear than by ambition or positive gains. Unfortunate as this is, such is the reality that we face. You can choose to ignore this or you can use this to your advantage. Here are some keywords you can use to relate to fear:

Future	Harm	Loss	Regret
Change	Ill Health	Enemy	Ruin

7) Greed and Sloth

Everyone is inherently lazy, me included. We want to laze around in a hammock by a nice white beach, reading a good book or spending some quality time with our loved ones. Who wants to work if we do not have to? Everybody wants a quicker, faster and easier way to do things. And that is why this trigger is so powerful and universal. It applies to *everybody*.

Greed Stimulants			
Free	Easy	Instant	Fast
WITHOUT* doing anything you don't like or don't want to do			
Key word: Without			

POSITIONED SELLING

And before I end this chapter, let me introduce a very powerful method for selling – I term it Positioned Selling. This moves you away from the traditional salesman route, into a consultant route. You are essentially doing the same thing, but the processes and media you use is totally different.

Basically, you will use the power of supply and demand to prove and generate further demand. Even if you are not really busy, just by looking busier, being less accessible and/or even increasing your prices will increase the demand for and appreciation of your services. Always remember, "Nobody goes to the guru at the bottom of the mountain."

The basics of implementing systems is to restrict your customers' direct access to you, but to require them to go through one or a combination of the below processes:
1) A questionnaire
2) Screening and pre-sale by your assistant
3) Booking for telephone appointments
4) Sending a box of marketing materials, such as books, checklists, videos, testimonials to highly qualified customers.

All the processes listed above will help to reinforce your position as a professional consultant, and the advantage this will provide is that by the time your customer actually reaches you, there is no longer any price resistance, or doubts about the quality of your services. You will only need to reconfirm what your processes have told them so far. Yes, it is more work than just quickly buying a media and sending out the marketing message, but this processes greatly increases conversion efficiency so that you can run successful campaigns in more advertising media.

Once you have built a reinforced position with processes and media, you can start using the below 5 major disqualifiers. This will reduce the number of unsuitable clients, pre-selecting only the best clients for you to work with.

1. Do they have the money?
2. Do they have an urgent and immediate problem?
3. Do you have a unique selling proposition that people want?
4. Do they have the ability to say yes?
5. Do your selling proposition fit in with their overall plans?

The above 5 disqualifiers can also be used for crafting your advertising message, as explained later in the Chapter 7. However, be cautioned that if done inappropriately, this can lead to poorer response rates, due to a more stringent criteria, though you will have higher quality leads. The best way to find out which is more profitable is to find ways to test cheaply, which I will explain in Part IV.

A Fundamental Choice

It is merely a matter of choice whether to use Positioned Selling or not. Note, that this choice will greatly affect how you are going to go through your career and what kind of experience it will be for you and your customers or clients. Positioned Selling is not only beneficial for you, but it also helps to create a much better customer experience. This is also significant added value as your customers will feel that they are privileged and special, as they are a part of an elite group who does business with you.

You will also work with more energy and enthusiasm, inject more creativity to your clients' project, and derive a more rewarding daily experience.

CHAPTER 7:

9 RULES OF RADIATION MARKETING™

Here are 9 rules you must always adhere when doing any form of paid advertising so as to maximize your dollars. As you create more advertisements, you will get complacent and forget. Hence, I urge to make it into a checklist you go through every time you write an ad. At the core of Radiation Marketing™, my unique marketing methodology, is to get people to respond to your advertisement, so that your overall cost of marketing is lower.

RESPONSE

Do you like to play a game with no rules? It might be fun, but it's a mess. Try having a mess on your deposit slip. It's simply not profitable, but that's what you are trying to do if you do not judge response.

Every time you visit someone as a consultant, you should aim to achieve a measurable outcome from the visit. Whether you are giving a follow-up call or sending more information to keep in constant contact. Because if getting a response is not your aim, then you will become a professional visitor. Do not be a professional visitor, because you are wasting your effort and marketing dollars.

Everything paid for should be doing what it is expected to be doing, including your season greetings card, because it is still meeting with your clients on your behalf. I'm sure you would expect your delivery man to be delivering goods, accountant to be doing accounts and marketing materials to be doing marketing.

Types of Response

When you are sending marketing materials out, it could be a direct purchase offer, Lead Generation offer or a mixture of the both. You should always aim to have a free offer to go along with the low priced direct purchase offer. Whatever it is, you must have a funnel in place to put your new leads in, to start building up trust. Only then, can you have a steady stream of leads slowly nurturing to supply you with a constant stream of buying customers all the time.

Low Threshold Offers

MAJOR POINT: You must always have low threshold offers available.

So what is threshold resistance? This is the amount of effort and discomfort required for people to come into your funnel at any stage. Ideally, there should be many entry points, each for different customers who are at a different stage of making their buying decision.

This is where your lead generation cores come in to attract people to enter your funnel. For example, a direct download, leaving a free email before the download, call in for a free trial, or fix a sales appointment for a paid trial.

You must ALWAYS have a very low threshold offer so that you can also capture those who are at very early points of the buying decision. For example:

1) Start with an instant free download for them to use immediately.
2) Then perhaps offer a video training series in exchange for their contact information at the end of the free download.
3) Next, you can offer a heavily discounted trial offer between $10 to $50, which should be almost at your cost price, or even lower if you can afford it.

Do you see how this can create tremendous value and build trust almost instantly? This is the fastest and easiest way to sell anything. See the Ascension Ladder Action Guide in the Gold Member's Area for more specific details.

Give them what they WANT

Also, note that you must advertise what they WANT. Do not try to convince people of what they need. It is very difficult and inefficient. You should try to convince people that you have what they want. See the difference? They already want your product and services, if only it works as they think it does. Hence, all you need to do is to build up trust, and they become your customer.

If you need to convince them to want your product, you would have doubled your work.

Do not sell, let them buy

Another point to note here is that people do not want to be sold. What this means is that do not keep pushing the features of your products and services. Let people choose how and if they want to receive your marketing messages at all. Only when they do, then you can start telling them about the benefits they will receive from your product. Remember, don't focus on your product features, but on the benefits that they will receive.

People who choose to respond to your advertisements are a lot more likely to buy, and this should be the group you engage. However, you must also give them the option to stop receiving your messages so that they can quickly change their mind for any reason at all.

Multiple Reasons and Channel of Responding

This is also an important aspect of designing an advertisement. People all have very different needs and preferences.

This can be related to the point of low threshold offers, but this is in the horizontal aspect rather than the vertical aspect. For example, car buyers will probably start from requesting brochures before requesting test drives. These are vertical aspects of the offer.

The horizontal aspect will be to give them other reasons to respond, such as coming in for a free car wash and check out the new cars at the same time. Or perhaps, you can channel the prospects from this other reason to respond directly into the car servicing part of your business. You get the point. If you put in some thought, I'm sure there are some other horizontal aspects of your business that you can easily provide and still yields a reasonable return for your extra work.

By the same reasoning, you should also provide them all the different ways to respond to the same advertisement, like email, text messages, voice or even Skype, for cross country sales. This will probably result in an extra 10% to 20% responses, but since you are spending money, might as well maximize it.

URGENCY

One big hidden cost of advertising lies with the almost persuaded. They see your advertisement, are interested but then they think, "Hmmm, maybe later." There are a million reasons why they want to put it off, but it is our job as consultants to help people make the decision to make their lives better, by taking action now!

This will have to be done by what I call Urgency Devices - Limited supply, limit per buyer, countdown clock, whatever. You need to structurally provide urgency to create stampede effect. In a live seminar, there is nothing more powerful than this live demonstration of people rushing to purchase stuff from you.

In the online world, you can still create the same effect, although you probably have to put in some extra thought to create a variation of the same devices I have mentioned.

INSTRUCTIONS

People do not like to purchase things when they are unclear of what is going to happen. It makes them feel uncomfortable, and it may stall or even kill the deal. You will need to give clear instructions on what they should expect at every step along the way.

For example, you should include a "What to expect at your first Appointment / Lesson / Trial" check list. Be sure to be clear, by including the relevant pricing, phone numbers, name of person to call, timing to call, venue of the location and other forms of communication that they may require.

Then repeat the instructions if you need to, perhaps in different medium. For example, first have them redirected to a page with the instructions, then allow them to download a pdf with the instructions, then at the same time also have an email and a phone text message containing the instructions and then you can still have the pdf instructions attached within both mediums. Sounds excessive? Not really, because you really should allow your customer the most convenient way to understand and contact you. It is simply good customer service, and trust me, you will get rewarded for it.

ACCOUNTABILITY

Management by objectives is the only way to manage and people needs to know and be accountable for the objectives that is allocated to them.
Good decisions always comes from timely relevant data, but the balance you will have to seek is with the cost factor.

Employees might be too lazy to track accurately, and it is your job as a business owner to create systems where you can quickly and affordably check whether your employees have been implementing the processes you have designed.
Usually a closed circuit television system is sufficient to ensure accountability. You might think this lowers employee morale, but it has been my experience that hardworking and diligent employees do not mind, and may even welcome such systems, because it weeds out the lazy employees, which will actually reduce their workload. However, you will need to prepare for initial resistance, and some staff might even resign. But this is good, as it will make your organization leaner and more profitable going forward.

You can also use gift with appointment to track and see how many appointments your staff has had. Or perhaps you can tie offer and promotion code to different advertisements so that you can track individual promotional campaigns. Many business owners also use coupon downloads for customers to redeem a free gift or trial, capturing customer information at the same time. Ideally, this should be the case for all marketing campaigns, as you will not only be able to account for every sale or trial offered, but will also be able to continue marketing to them at the same time.

In any case, make sure you track every advertisement campaign and make it accountable for the sales it is supposed to generate for you. If it is not profitable, either improve it, or scrap it altogether, no matter what it costs you to create the campaign. Once in a while, you will create what you think will be a huge winner, but turned out to be a complete flop. Do not waste time; just cut it and move on. Hence, for businesses who wants to get the most from their marketing budget, its best to test fast, so that you can fail fast and move on to your next, possibly winning, campaign.

FREE BRAND BUILDING

You should build your brand as a result of direct response and not the other way round. This will allow you to build your brand for free, while still giving your brand a meaning.
Many small companies try to imitate what large companies do and promote their brand, which does not yet have a meaning that consumers can understand. This is like saying a meaningless thing in a pretty way, which wastes a ton of money. Unless you have a huge marketing budget and an established brand, this is not recommended. There are many other much more effective ways to build a brand. You should also note that those large companies also did not grow to what they are now with brand advertising. Your brand should say something about the quality or uniqueness of your product, and there are no better ways to do this than by way of direct response advertising.

Some companies now even do naked advertisement, enticing customers to some benefits before revealing their association, or even entirely based on curiosity before revealing benefits and association. This gives more meaning to their brand, as it presents the solutions and benefits first before even revealing themselves.

Another good way to build your brand is to link it with specific complementary benefits, such as health for food processors or prestige with cars, and you will create lasting impression in people. Such is the position that many luxury car companies have adopted, resulting in the ability to sell their cars for many times over its cost. Another good example is the George Foreman grill, incorporating a healthier choice benefit into a BBQ grill, when grills and healthy eating used to be mutually exclusive.

The important thing is, you don't have to break the bank to build a meaningful brand.

FOLLOWING UP

Where there is no follow up, you can view it exactly as though money has just been flushed down the toilet bowl. I'm sure most business owners are very averse to this idea, so why are most people too slothful to follow up? Yes, it is time consuming, and that's why you will need to have a proper system to follow up efficiently! If you are unable to think of a system or you require technical expertise to design a cheap and easy-to-use follow up mechanism, do take me up on my Platinum or Titanium Membership options!

Follow Up Mechanisms
In Singapore, the few main follow up mechanisms are:

1. Direct Call
   This takes time, and it could be a nuisance to people unless they fall into the hot prospect category – Those who are ready to buy, and wish to do so quickly. They would appreciate your call and this is the absolute best method to follow up if you have prospects in this category.
   However, I would not recommend to use this method of follow up for warm leads, as there are better ways to keep in touch with your warm leads. Warm leads require more information from you before deciding, and its more convenient for them to receive information from you via email or a link to your website, hence this is a much better way to follow up with warm leads.

2. Text Messages
   This is the next most intrusive way to follow up, after a direct phone call, and you can probably send text messages only once a week for pure follow up purpose, unless your prospect replies to your message. However, text messages have a very high read rate, as almost all people reads their text messages, especially those sent via SMS.

   Hence, this is a good way to follow up with warm leads, as sometimes your clients are too busy to take calls and would prefer to reply messages at their own convenience. The text limitation in messages also indicates that you should include a web link so that your prospects can access more information.

   If you have a large pool of contacts, you can and should attempt to segment them into groups such as buyers or none buyers, or buyers of a certain product and so on. If you are able to do segmentation, you need to use the Excel filter function combined with Google contact or any other fast and easy method for you to easily import contact from CSV files into your phone. Because of the dynamic nature of this following up, you cannot be keying in customers' contacts individually. It would be a poor use of time.

3. Email
   Email follow up is so powerful because there is unlimited real estate there, and you can use text, audio *and* video to reach your customer, limited only by their time and interest in you. And best of all, you can set-up automatic follow up mechanisms so you only have to do the work once!
   Hence, you must try your very best to offer plenty of incentive for people to join your mailing list. Generic single free reports might not be enough now that so many people are doing it.

   Currently, a 3 video training series, plus cheat sheets, will probably pull in the most opt-ins, but it requires more work than just sitting on your computer and typing. Later in Chapter 10, I discuss a few different types of video you can use, and their pros and cons.

4. Advertisement re-targeting
   Ideally, you should reduce this form of following up as much as possible, because it is the most expensive of the 4 follow up methods, and it also means that you failed to capture their email or phone number so that you can follow up more directly. Over time, this could cost a lot, and should be reduced as much as possible. This is usually done via Google and Facebook, through paid advertisement methods. And that's the reason why you will need to make sure that your website opt-in rate is as high as possible, so that you can follow up as often as you need and sending whatever content you need to send, at almost zero cost.

Situations for Follow Up

Below are a few example of situations where follow up is lacking, and systems MUST be put in place to stem the loss of these opportunities. It is all money slipping right through your palms.

1. Inbound caller where contact information is not captured, and hence stays unknown and received no follow up
2. Little or no follow up on leads at trade or consumer show
3. Inadequate follow up to ask or request for referrals
4. Instant follow up to new customers
5. Prevention or rescue related to lost customers

How to Follow Up?

Below is a standard sequence you can use for following up, by offering the same thing again, to slight variations, to a totally different kind of solution. You can also skip some steps if you want, but EXECUTE your follow up.

1. Restate, resell and re-extend the same offer
2. Stern or humorous notice, emphasizing on rushing dateline
3. Deadline and disappearance of offer
4. Extend payment – Offer longer payment period or different mode of payment
5. Change product type – Offer a cheaper model of the car
6. Offer alternatives solution for the same problem – For example, if they wanted a car, now offer them a van.

DISREGARD APPEARANCE

The end result of your self-designed marketing piece might look like an infomercial, but don't worry, because it works. However, there's no saying that you cannot combine looks with functionality. However, you would have to spend a little more on improving the design portion to create a profitable marketing message.

RESULTS ONLY

And by what exactly do I mean by results? It must be a measurable objective, where you get people to *do something*. People are only interested if they choose to invest their time and/or money to interact with you. Don't be a professional visitor, where you only show up, say, "Hi" and then leave. You're wasting your time. Only results in terms of direct purchases or email sign-ups or call-ins where they leave their phone number or anything tangible count. If you are merely brand building, you are only making business a lot more difficult than it needs to because marketing just became a lot more expensive.

In order to achieve good results, there is no need to reinvent the wheel. You merely have to look around and see what features, phrases and bonuses others in the industry use and tweak them to suit your own business. Look especially for those advertisements which have longevity, because no business owners would run the same ad month over month if it is not profitable.

If you are using internet marketing such as Twitter and Facebook, you need to beware of the new metrics nonsense. Just because you got thousands of "Likes" does not mean you made a single cent. Likewise, making thousands of dollars does not mean you definitely get 100 "Likes". Where do you want to be at? If you chose the latter, good for you! But in order to get there, you need to hold whatever media you are using responsible for delivering results. Only then, can you test and improve, and finally move on to use the Unlimited Traffic Technique, further explained in Chapter 17.

ABSOLUTE ADHERENCE

There must be no deviation from the designated marketing plan and the Radiation Marketing rules. Or at least until you are making a comfortable profit.

1. **Purge the junk**
   You might already have lots of marketing material which you find that does not really work. Stop using them as your main marketing material! Instead, use them as supplementary materials to include along with your new Direct Marketing materials. This way, you can achieve brand building, without incurring additional distribution costs

2. **Decide on a new marketing plan**
   If you have not designed a new marketing plan using the attached Radiation Marketing Action Plan, it's time to start! I have mentioned earlier in this book, and it is so important that I will mention it again. The magic of this book is in the application of it! Get the marketing plan done now!

3. **Start counting and measuring**
   Counting and measuring is so important because the very act of increases clarity. You will find out exactly what to measure, and why is it so important to measure it. As you see the figures clearly in front of you, you will naturally decide to improve the figures, until a point where you feel that it is acceptable. This is also the only way for you to test and improve the performance of your advertisement's conversion rates.

4. **Build marketing mind muscle**
   You will need to learn how to properly use the different platforms in order to maximize their effectiveness. For example, Google Adwords used to be really cheap and you can practically make money on any keywords you are using, but now that method will get you killed. You might rack up thousands of dollars in advertising cost, with no idea how to pay them off. Now, you should at least acquire a moderate level of Google Adwords knowledge before you go into the battlefield.

You should also start learning more about direct marketing. Copywriting, list building, consumer psychology and money math are some of the fields you should really know about when it comes to building profitable marketing campaigns!

5. **Get some good tools**
   Good tools will help you learn in the most effective way, saving you hours of precious time.
   You can also purchase or build up your copywriting banks of power words and emotion triggering phrases to get your prospects eating out of your hand! Control their actions as you would your own hands if you use the right language and give the right solutions that helps your prospects solve their problem.

6. **Be alert and resistant**
   There are many who dissuade and distract from direct marketing, suggesting not to follow the rules stated in this chapter. It might be because this is not the way they were taught to do things or perhaps they are not comfortable with the very idea of it. But you have to take care to stick carefully to these tested and proven rules because all successful marketers knows: Doing it this way delivers results.

There you have it, 10 rules of Radiation Marketing that you will have to adhere to in order to ensure that your advertisement is the leanest and cheapest. Look at it as a checklist of specific items to check through when you have finished writing the advertisement.

And I can see your next question coming: But how do I even write the advertisement in the first place? There are basically 2 overarching concepts that you can use, the PAIS or the AIDA. They are quite similar, but I like to offer choices. You should too: People always like to choose what they want.

PROBLEM, AGITATE, INVALIDATE, SOLVE (PAIS)

People buy things to solve problems. They buy beauty products because they want to become prettier, books because they want to be smarter and so on. One product can solve many problems though, so it is up to you which problem you want to angle towards helping your customers solve. You can just buy a simple table if you only need a place to do your work, but some people might want a custom made, ergonomic table, specifically designed to do a certain type of paperwork, and this is how you can differentiate your product. Every product has its own features, including color, which you can turn it into a benefit to create value for your customers

1. **Problem**
   Define the problem! What is the biggest problem, that drives your prospect to seek a solution immediately?
   Let's take learning guitar as an example. There are those who just want to learn music, but it's much more likely that they want to learn it for a specific reason, for example, to impress their first date.

   Most average copywriters would've phrased the "problem" in a superficial manner. For example, "Want to learn guitar? This beginner course will get playing in days!" That's like saying the reason a man buys a drill is because he doesn't have a drill.

   Try this instead "Girls ignoring you? Learn to live with it OR impress them with your guitar prowess. Find out here: [enter your link]

   Always narrow down the problem to ensure that it will appeal to a specific group who wants your product for a solution to a specific problem. This is the group of customers who are likely to act immediately.
   The key is to understand your customer. You CAN'T define the problem successfully without first knowing your customer and their basic problems. It's simply impossible.

2. Agitate

Now that you have a problem, make the problem a little bigger so that it's easier to incite action. Note that there are no actual, physical changes, only the state of mind of the prospect changes when you do this. You could add a paragraph like this:

"Girls ignoring you?

Just trying to find a nice woman that you can wake up to everyday? That will never happen until she thinks you are a man. And that day will NEVER come unless you do something about it …

Learn to live with it OR impress them with your guitar prowess. Find out here: [enter your link]

See the difference? Adding the paragraph makes them quickly relive the pain, that they probably want to avoid in the future.

3. Invalidate

So now that your prospect know that they have a problem, and that they want to solve it fast, they need a solution. But why should they choose you over, let's say a competitor with a stronger branding?

If your products or services are truly unique, then you there is no need for this step. However, chances are they are not. Hence, you need to give them reasons saying why you are different.
In most cases, you are not dealing with 1st time customers. They likely have already purchased something promising the same thing, but without the results they desired.

That is why you do not want customers to see you as part of the crowd, but as a different solution to the same problem.
Having a strong USP will help, and having a power Lead Generating core, like a free trial or eBook will really help a lot to build trust, and get customers to contact you instead.

4. **Solve**

Here, you can finally present a solution. Your lead generating core could be a teaser, leading up to a purchase offered here as the complete solution to their problems.

Or perhaps, the lead generation core is what you would like them to download at this stage, in exchange for their email. And the download plus the email will lead them to the eventual purchase.

One great presentation style is to stack up benefits, translating the time or money saved into an actual, reasonable amount. Then chisel away the price, giving reasons why you want to bring down the price, so that the already great value becomes an irresistible steal at the reduced price.

You can further compare it with a different category of product. For example, audio programs can be compared to live seminars, or juicing machines can be compared to pricey exercise equipment. This helps customers justify the purchase, even if it is higher than the normal price for its category of products.

Then, make the solution easy to purchase, by offering strong guarantees, or have a lower priced version so that they can trial your products first. And if they still do not want it, channel them to perhaps another delivery method. For example, some people prefers seminar style approach to learning, while others prefer a hands on Activity based styles.

Think through what you can offer, and have the mindset that it is your duty to provide them with a solution. Don't end just before offering them something to buy, or even if they are not buying at the moment. You must always have a "What's next?" You mentioned a problem, then give them a solution. Once you gave them a solution, then offer a more detailed, more comprehensive, perhaps a done for you version of the solution. Then perhaps you can offer them another product which can be used to complement the solution that was already purchased. I hope you can see that you should always have another "What's next?" planned for them right from the start. This is how you create value, and ensure that your business grows continuously, without taking a break.

ATTENTION, INTEREST, DESIRE, ACTION! (AIDA)

This is another model that you can use as the overall concept when you are writing your advertisement. Personally, I prefer the PAIS approach, because it is more direct and customer oriented, but to each his own.

1. **Attention**

    In the current media-filled world, you need to be quick to grab people's attention. Use powerful words or pictures that will grab the reader by the throat or heavily pique their curiosity to make them stop and read what you have to say next.

    Good openers addresses their problems and begin with such as:

    Do you ever...?
    Have you noticed...?
    Warning: ...?
    Who else wants...?

    Bad openers gives reader something to object to or just bore them to tears:

    I've got just the thing you want...?
    I just dropped by to...?
    I was wondering if you could...?

    It's simply not powerful enough to make them want to know more.

2. **Interest**

    This is a challenging stage: You've got their attention, but can you engage with them enough to spend their precious time understanding your message in more detail?

Gaining the reader's interest is a deeper process than grabbing their attention. You have a little more time to do it, but stay focused on their needs. Use bullets, subheadings, highlights and bold type to break up the text to help them quickly pick out the relevant messages.

Here are some points you can use:
- Listening to their problems (For a live presentation)
- Telling them about your experience on things that affect their problems.
- Getting them actively involved, perhaps by giving them a time or money savings calculator

The #1 Marketing Sin is being boring. Never bore your readers: Entertain them by using funny, appealing, colorful, interesting, ideally pictures and videos, to bring your point about your products across.

3. Desire

People can recognize that they have a need, but without desire they still will not act. Desire is a motivation to act and leads towards the next stage.

At this point, you want to create desire in your interested customers to have your product by appealing to their personal needs and wants. You must turn the story you've told into one that is not only extremely relevant to the prospect, but also irresistible. A unique selling point will help customers desire it over competitor products.

Desire is like a fire, which you should stoke by as many methods as you can:
- Showing them how your product or services will not be available for long (Scarcity principle).
- Showing how other people approve of the item and have acquired and used it successfully themselves. (Proof and Testimonials: Videos, Photos and Text)

- Showing them how what you have to offer will solve some of their problems. (Demonstration: The more dramatic, the deeper impression you make.)

4. Action

And at the end of it all, is where they take action on their desires and buy the product or agree to your proposals.

You can summarize the problem and explanation of how you will solve it.

The main task at this stage is to make the purchase as simple as possible, by offering a range of payment options and avenues. For example, you can offer cash, credit card, cheque or PayPal payment terms, with a one-time investment or a 3 time installment option, plus a powerful 1 month no questions asked money back guarantee, or a 1 year "I used it, but I don't like it" buyback program. And if there is still no action, follow up with a lower priced version or different delivery method of the product.

At the risk of repeating myself, here's a final short summary of how to write a great advertisement:

Always start with customer interest, desire and fear before revealing the solution tied to your business
1. Write to and for the psyche of the customer
2. Write **emotionally** and not factually
3. Be bold and overemphasize on the claims and promises
4. Always have an offer, urgency and clear instructions

---

* Action Time!

Start creating the draft for your first advertisement! Use Word or PowerPoint to write down the headlines, main points as well as the offer price and options. You will still have to reformat it for the specific media you want to be using, so there's no need for perfection.

Also, start to create or find good eye catching or appealing pictures that you can use for your advertisement later on. ~

CHAPTER 8:

25 TRUST FLARES

If you look at it closely, people are really paying a premium for trust. Why do you buy the brand that you usually buy? Why do people follow doctor's advice closely? Though in general, trust in doctors or people in general are generally decreasing due to the internet, which I will discuss later in this chapter.

You need to create and leverage high Trust from which you can build equity, from which you can create value and extract money from at the same time.

It's a fact: Trust sells.

It's about having the other guy's back all of the time, staying interesting and useful throughout the years. Messages conveyed by untrusted people are greatly devalued, as compared to those coming from a trusted person. This is especially important in B2B sales, because each sales cycle may take 1 month to 1 year, and building trust is especially important. However, trust is a funny thing, because much undeserved trust occurs, and sometimes it can be gained in very superficial ways. For example if you are overseas, and you meet someone from the same country or city, you will naturally trust that person more. But logically speaking, he or she is still a stranger that you do not really know.

People do not have confidence in selecting people to trust and they distrust themselves around sales people, so the mind automatically looks for shortcut about whom to place trust in. I have made a list of these shortcuts which can be found under the **Trust Triggers** section later in this chapter

First let us look at 4 common mistakes regarding trust that business owners make, followed by a few methods for destroying trust.

4 COMMON MISTAKES

1. Business owners frequently underestimate the skepticism and the high level of investment required for customer acquisition. Marketing messages must be crafted with the understanding that recipients will be stubbornly reluctant to believe them.

2. You have to understand that every customer will have different angles from which they want the same product that you are selling. For example, a weight loss product targeted at ladies might have a customer who want to lose weight for a high school reunion, another because she wants to stay healthy, and yet another because she wants to keep her husband's eyes from straying. Inadequate preparation for the sales appointment can result in the prospect not hearing what she wants, and this will greatly reduce the chance that the prospect will buy.

3. Acting based on assumptions rather than facts. Especially the assumption that just because your think you have superior products, people will trust you. Truth is, don't count on it. You need to establish trust, before they buy, *then* you can depend on product superiority for your customers to continue to stick with you.

4. Hastily creating advertising without research, tested and proven models or copywriting skills, that builds trust quickly and easily. Trust is not easy to get, and that's why proven models and skills are absolutely essential.

METHODS TO KILL TRUST

Below are a few methods that will erode the trust that your customers have in you; you will do well to make sure you reduce the below as much as possible. You will notice the below are signs that scream "Salesman!". It is not an exhaustive list, so avoid displaying any other common signs to your prospects as well.

1) Shelf of trophies, wall of plagues or equivalent
2) Too easily and readily accessible
3) Too pliable
4) Too eager
5) Being pushy
6) Obviously trying to hurry the prospect
7) Overconfident and glib, with a quick answer to everything
8) Pushing products when you should be diagnosing needs and offering custom solutions
9) Evading or altering questions

THE ULTIMATE TRUST DESTROYER

Google is a great tool for people nowadays in their search for information. Yet there is no bigger way to kill trust than this. When your prospect says he "needs to think about it" and goes home to do his "due diligence" by searching for the generic name of your product or service, it blows the trust you have built up into a million pieces. They see so many similar products and services, and sometimes they become overwhelmed and then they do not buy. Or it commoditizes your products and services that customers start to bargain on price.

When customers reach a stage where they want to do their due diligence, you know you have made a wrong move in your presentation, because you just gave them some information that they have heard before, and that they want to check it out.

The best way to combat this Trust Destroyer is to re-brand and re-name your product. By having a specific and unique name for your product, when customers reach this stage where they want to do their 'due diligence, all they find is you and your materials because of the specific and unique name that they searched for. This is the power of branding used correctly, because you have positioned yourself so differently from all your competitors.

25 TRUST FLARES

These are factors that will help you to gain trust from your prospects. Below is quite a comprehensive, though by no means exhaustive, list.

Affinity – If your prospects or customers feel that they have something in common with you, they will naturally trust you. For example, if both you and your prospect are both dog lovers and like to listen to the same song and likes to eat similar types of food, wouldn't this make you trust the person more so than someone whose not? This is one of the power points in marketing, selling and networking, and you should use it as often as you can in your marketing materials. It simply conjures trust easily where there is none!

Authenticity – This helps your prospects answer this question – "Is this guy for real?" People need to know if you walk the talk and whether you say what you mean, rather than just being another pliable salesman. To achieve this, you have to portray a consistent image across all channels of communication that you offer. One slip, if not recovered properly, and people start to feel that you are just fluff.

Authority – People in authority positions gains other people's trust more easily. Such authority can be granted by government organization, by ways of their position in a company or it simply be manufactured by writing a book or making quality video content that other people trust. Social proof also contributes to making you an authority.

Believability – Most people are usually equipped with the thinking that if it is too good to be true, it probably is. For example, let's say you have an offer which says that you are giving out free Ice Cream. Instantly, people will think "Why is that guy doing that?". However, if you add a second line which says "Opening Special" or "Building Awareness for Charity Fundraiser", it becomes a lot more palatable for your prospective customers.

Having a good reason why you are doing a promotion always increases response rates.

Celebrity – The reason that celebrity endorsements are so powerful is that celebrities draw attention simply by having their pictures there. Naturally, people will draw the conclusion that if such an influential person is rooting for this product, then it must be a great product. This can also be used if you have influential people as your customers. These are what we call cache clients. Just letting people know they are your customers will greatly boost your trust level.

Comfort - If people feel comfortable with you they will trust you more. Do not give them too much pressure when selling to them, rather stay at the top of their mind with constant contact, either via email Facebook or even phone text messages, but never make them feel pressured and they will grow to become lifetime customers, the most valuable asset you can ever have. You can also make customers feel more comfortable by telling them clearly what you are offering, so that they feel that they are making an informed decision about you.

Consistency – You have to do what you say. If you say you are going to give 5 tips for increasing traffic, for example, then you must give 5. More is fine, but never less. If you say that there is something that you do, make sure that you never give evidence of situations which can prove otherwise.

Credibility – You can also think of trust as a function of credibility. This can be augmented via additional positioning assets to help boost your authority, and make others feel that you are knowledgeable and competent about your industry. This helps others quickly decide: Can this person be trusted?

Customized Solutions - Despite the fact that the same solution will solve all 10 people's problems, most people think that their problems are unique. Hence, you should always provide customized solutions to help people make a quicker and more trusted decision. Providing a customized solution via a Diagnose and Prescribe method works the best. This also shows that you are listening to what your customers are saying, and this automatically creates more trust than if you were just peddling – selling the same thing to everyone.

Demonstration – There are few better and easier ways to build trust than a demonstration. Especially if it is dramatic.
A DRAMATIC demonstrations is when you show that your products work as mentioned in a very amazing way. You can also attach a serious consequence to the demonstration so that it becomes dramatic.
Houdini is a great example. Magicians in his and even our time consider him to be just average in his skills as a magician. However, his dramatic emphasis when performing his tricks added a gigantic "wow" factor, which led to his longevity even till today. His performance of the straightjacket escape tricks hanging from the air, upside down, above the audience and frequent escapes from prisons are some of the many dramatic demonstrations of his skills. Many magicians of his time also knew and were able to do what he did, but this difference in the dramatic presentation of skills and knowledge created a huge difference.

Endorsements - If you manage to get endorsements from a well-known person in your field, or even if they are not well known by a large number of people, then this will help you to become trusted by others as well. LinkedIn has this specific endorsements in skills by other people, and hence this can be an easy way for you to start building up your endorsements from friends and family.

Exclusivity – If you already attained celebrity and expert status, you can still further increase trust by being exclusive. By only allowing certain people to have access to an exclusive product further increases the trust. Remember, nobody goes to the guru at the bottom of the mountain right? Reducing your availability greatly builds up time sensitivity, and this also helps people to learn to value your time by only being concise and to the point. Kind of like killing 2 birds with one stone, because you can now charge more while completing things faster.

Frequency - Frequent *and* useful communication from you to your customers is also a great way to build trust. That's why doing product launches (Series of informative or training video, leading up to the offer of the final product for sale) are so successful, because it creates anticipation at the next upcoming video, if the first video is useful and informative. Video is the undisputed best way to do marketing, aside from perhaps a good live presentation, because of its multi-sensory outputs and versatility. I explain more about product launches in Chapter 10.

Feasibility of Relationship – Your prospect must feel like they are able to work with you. They need to feel that your working style is similar to theirs, or at the very least acceptable for them to work with. If your client prefers to work with a quieter personality, you should adjust your appearance and tone down, even if you are a chatty person. In NLP, this is also known as mirroring. You can also view this through the Affinity aspect: People trust and like to work with others who are like themselves.

Language – No, I don't mean this in terms of the language spoken in different country. Though that will help in building trust as well, but here I am referring to the lingo or technical terms that people in that field uses. For example, to relate to stockbrokers doing technical analysis you will need to use terms like MACD, TEMA and VPT so your target market will feel that you are like them, and that you understand them. This is very important for building trust.

Leadership Position – Leadership position can give you a huge advantage as the biggest and the best in town when you are creating trust and it allows for premium pricing as well. Many affluent people can and will pay extra to work with the leader in the market, because their time is so precious, and not worth the time and hassle to check around for the best deal. They just want the best service out there, even if it is more expensive. For example, Hertz have been a leader in the car rental market for a long time, Avis comes in second and they are in a good position so it will probably stay that way for some time to come.

However, defending this position can prove to be more expensive than it is worth, and sometimes you might have to walk away from this position altogether.

An excellent example to quote here is Domino's and their Leadership Position of hot, fresh pizza in 30 minutes or less. When they tried to roll it out nationwide, increasing delivery accidents and skyrocketing insurance costs forced them to give up this position.

You have to keep in mind of this danger that when it becomes no longer profitable to hold the leadership position, you have to be prepared to walk away from it.

Longevity – If you have been in the market for over hundreds of years, your company will naturally become a trusted brand. But not to worry, this is not the only way, neither is it the best way to position yourself for maximal trust. But if you have been in your market place for several years to a few decades, why not use it?

Place – Locating yourself in a premium location also helps to increase trust. This is the reason why many companies choose to locate themselves in prominent business districts, though it costs a lot more. This helps them to secure much trust than they would if they were located in a shady location.

Second Party Transferal – This is an excellent way to build trust, much in the same way referred customers are the best customers you can have. Most likely the second party is a satisfied customer, and have already pre sold the referred customer, so they are merely confirming if you are someone they want to work with, rather than you having to go through the whole process to sell your company, building trust up from scratch. This is especially powerful if you have influential customers who will help to promote you.

NOT-a-Salesman Status – A salesman and a consultant are both essentially doing the same thing. They talk to other people and convince them to do something. However, the difference is that a consultant is a well sought after person, and this gives him power over the market. You just have to position yourself differently, and this will easily double your income. It's a lot of upfront work to do positioning, but it will definitely pay for the cost of itself many times over. The last section in Chapter 6, on Positioned Selling explains this in detail.

Proof – The reason this is so powerful is that people know that others like themselves have tried and experienced your products and services and benefited greatly. The more the merrier, there is no such thing as too many customer testimonials or reviews from others. However, let's go deeper into the different levels of proof that your customers will need to buy your product. Here are the 4 levels of proof, and the question that your prospects will ask in their mind, which you should answer (in advance, if possible) before they dismiss the thought and just walk away.

When you get customer testimonial, it will be good to have at least 1 that addresses proof at each level.

1) Proof of Concept
   "Does this thing even work?"

2) Proof of Need
   "Even if the product does work, do I need it?"

3) Proof of Outcome
   "Even if I did need it, will I get the outcomes as described?"

4) Proof of Superiority
   "Even if it could deliver the said outcomes, is this the best out there?"

It might seem a little paranoid to think so deeply into the customer buying mind set. But in truth, people do think through all the above 4 points very quickly, when making buying decisions, that they might not even be conscious of it. Do not underestimate the need for a wide variety and quantity of customer reviews and testimonials required.

Risk reversal – In most situations, people pay prior to experiencing your goods and services, and this presents a risk to the customer. The higher the price, the larger the risk and this will greatly affect your sales, as there is a significant hurdle to overcome to even try. And since people are motivated more by the fear of loss than the ambition for gain, you can lose many customers who does not even want to try.

You have to make it really easy for people to try, or even offer a risk reversal. Try it for free. Try it for a small fee. Or pay nothing now, or pay only a percentage of what you save for them. Of course for different industry and different companies it varies how you should use this risk reversal technique for maximum profit, as your economics must support this before it can be a worthwhile trial. Otherwise you might end up losing money as you get more customers.

However, the point remains that you should allow trials, or guarantees so that customers feel the risk is on you, the business, and not on them as customers.

Safety – This is linked to risk reversal, although it's not exactly the same. You see, there are other ways for people to feel safe buying your product, for example you can say bring a friend to try too. Or that many people have already tried. It might seem similar to what we have already stated above, and to a certain extent, it is. But I hope this point can help you think outside the box and come up with different ideas for your customers to feel safe buying your product.

Superiority – You may have a product that is superior in every aspect to your competitor. However, just by being superior is not enough. You have to demonstrate that you really are superior, and so the form and method of communication that you are superior is very important. Sometimes all you have to do is to say you are superior and it will work. Other tines you have to give a short trial, and yet other times you have to give a long trial plus a powerful demonstration before it is enough. As again, the quantity required is all dependent on the how big is the ticket for your product.

Value – Providing exceptional value is an excellent way to build trust. This is why trials at a really low price can help your customers to start a relationship with you, and to experience for themselves the value you provide. Even if they feel that you are not within their expectations of a full priced products, at the trial price it could still be a steal, and they would walk away satisfied and still recommend friends to go for the trial if nothing else. And from there, once they have established the first contact, you can put them into your nurturing system to eventually convert them into long term customers. As again, the economics is very important, and you should structure the trial to allow you to still earn a small profit from every customer.

USING THE RIGHT TRUST BUILDING SALES TOOLS

The wrong tools will scream "Salesman!" to other people and shut them off before you even start. Let's take a look between what a normal salesman would use versus what you *should be* using. Yup, that's right, call yourself anything, but a salesman.

Salesman		Advisor, Coach, Consultant, Doctor, Expert
Brochure		Book
Slide Presentation	VS	Dialogue, Diagnoses, Prescription, Taking & Noting Points On Paper
Scripted Speech, Picking Up Where Left Off		Thoughtful Response
Products		Solutions
Tries To Close		Prescriptions And Action Plans To Make Them Buy

Fig 8.1 Using The Right Sales Tools

THE TIME MANUFACTURING MACHINE

No doubt, there is a lot of work to do in order to create lots of tools and materials to position yourself. But I assure you that it is worth the effort to go through it, so that you can live the life you have always dreamed about.

If you have always thought about buying time, this is as close as you can get.

It's a little unconventional, but look at it this way: Every time someone consumes your published material, whether they listen to your audio programs, see your video, read your book or your online articles, you are saving time from speaking to them, to convince them that you are the authority in your field, and in essence you would have manufactured time.

This is the best way to multiply selling your time, as compared to just depending on your job.

There is only a certain limit that you can go in improving your craft, so that you become an expert in your field. Any further financial compensation are usually dependent on who you are and your personality as a public figure, rather than what you do, and publishing contents and materials is the way to go.

In the next few chapters, I will be introducing the various types of sales tools that you should use to multiply your time, spread your personality and create massive trust.

CHAPTER 9:

TRUST TOOL - BOOKS

Author is in the word authority. Need I say more?

In this time and age, it is very easy to self-publish your own book, and it is still the undisputed way to build trust and establish your credibility. You book is a manifestation of you, walking around telling people how good you are without you having to do anything at all, after you have finished to book. An interesting way to look at a book is that it is a brochure that someone else pays for, and this brochure of you will likely be one of the best investments of time you can make.

Granted, it takes a lot of work to write the book, but there are plenty of ways to simplify it.

Here are a few ways to get your book writing started, as well as my quick background of self-publishing a book.

COMMITMENT TO WRITE YOUR OWN BOOK

What I thought would be a 20 day process turned out to take 5 months to complete, because I did not factor in the time you would need for research. I wanted to write a 200 page book at a speed of 10 pages a day. Based on my estimation that it takes me around 20 minutes to write a page, it would take me around 3 hours every day to complete the book in 20 days.

By my estimate, writing a book should be worth at least $10,000 in the 1st year alone, so if you divide it out, based on a 200 page book, each page is worth $50. And if you take 20 minutes to write a page, you would be making $150 in an hour! Based on a 20 8-hour workdays, this equates to a $24,000 monthly income, and this really helps in gluing my bum to the chair.

Not to mention the fame and status attached to having you own book which becomes a runaway success. Yes, this might only be a goal, but frequent visualization of this very compelling goal will help you to work towards it, or at the very least help you to finish you book. Your book does not need to be a huge hit to make you $10,000 by the way. This is probably the minimum you can make from your own book. If it did turn out to be a hit, you can probably make an easy $100,000 within 3 months. I hope this is motivation enough?

An additional tip is to keep the internet off when you are writing for minimal distraction possibilities. If you need to do research, make a list of items you will need to find, keeping this copy of research materials on hand. *Then* turn off the internet.

If you do not think that your book is worth $10,000 to you, there are only a few possibilities:
1) Your book lack content, because you lack knowledge, and hence you feel that it would not sell or promote you as well as it should.
   Solution: Sometimes people underestimate their own abilities, so you should get started writing your book anyway. If you truly lack the knowledge, it is unlikely you can fill up a 100 page book. Once you realize this, then you can start researching. This way, you become more knowledgeable and soon (usually less than a year if you are committed and interested) you will truly become qualified to write about the topic.

2) You have the knowledge, but you are unable to sell or monetize your book in a way that would be profitable.
   Solution: In the past, publishing a book takes lots of time and effort to find a publisher who would publish your own book, because they need to make sure that it would be profitable before incurring the cost. Nowadays, the cost of self-publishing is so low that aside from the time required to write your own

book, there isn't much other cost. You can publish your book with less than SGD $500, so it is pretty much impossible that you can't even recoup this amount of cost. There are many other ways of monetizing your book, which I describe later in this chapter. You might not recover the cost immediately, but you can be sure that it will pay for itself over time.

3) You are unable to find the commitment or it's not worth your time to write your own book. Though for the latter, it is pretty unlikely, as if you already have some measure of success without a book, then writing a book is very likely to add another digit to your earnings.

Solution 1: Speaking Your Book

Here is a shortcut to writing your book. Get a voice recorder and record what you want to write. The average person speaks around 120 and 180 words per minute per minute depending on the rhythm, style of speech, language, etc. Let's take an average of 150 words per minute, so in order to write book with around 150 pages, which will contain around 40,000 words, you will only need 4 to 5 hours' worth of things to talk about, and your content part would be done. Next, you will need to find an online transcribing service to convert the speech into texts, and then after some re-arrangement of your ideas and formatting of the book (CreateSpace provides both of these services) and voila! You now have your own book. Obviously, it is more expensive this way, as you have to pay for the transcribing and formatting services, but it saves a lot of time this way.

Solution 2: Ghostwriting Your Book

If you really do not have the passion to finish writing your own book, it might be better to just get a ghostwriter to do it, because it would save you a lot of time. This is definitely not the best idea, but at least you would get your own book at the end.

One of the main reason why many things fail is that they are never finished in the first place. Writing a own book is one of the many things.

You should still create the content backbone of the book before you outsource your project, and you should always read through the manuscript and re-write some parts of the books so that it would have your personality in it.

KNOWLEDGE TO WRITE YOUR BOOK

You cannot write a good quality book without sufficient knowledge about your own subject matter. You simply cannot have input without output, and hence I strongly advocate reading a minimum of a book a month on your specialized subject matter.

I read a book a week, and I still do not think I can keep up-to-date with all the current state of matters in my industry. If you lack time to sit down and read, get audio books, which you can listen to while commuting. This is one of the most powerful time creating method that absolutely everyone who wants to succeed should use.

If you have not already, go and find at least 20 audio programs and listen to them. There are many free ones on YouTube. From these, you should find 1 or 2 that really inspires you to wake up a little earlier, sleep a little later every day and really gets you moving. Listen to them 5 to 10 times, or ideally until you can almost give the speech yourself. Research has shown that you need to listen to the same thing multiple times, before you can internalize them as your own core values and greatly benefit from it.

Also, your book must not only contain plenty of valuable and relevant information, but it should be organized for easy understanding, recalling and usage for it to be a really compelling and highly recommended book. You can have all the knowledge in the world, but it does not help anyone if you are unable to use it or impart it to others. That is also the reason why I included so many action guides: So that people can use the guides and act upon the information they have just read. As I always say, knowledge is only potential power. Action turns it into real power.

CREATESPACE INDEPENDENT PUBLISHING PLATFORM

This is Amazon's self-publishing arm, and the power of this is that you get your book listed on Amazon.com. Amazon has built a very powerful distribution network, and through its logistical capabilities to quickly deliver both physical and digital books to any parts of the world, it has very significant market power

So much so that if your book is not on Amazon, people feel that it's probably not a good book. Many people also frequently research which books to read on Amazon, so it is the place where you absolutely need to get listed on.

HOW MUCH DOES IT COST?

It is actually quite cheap to get your books off the press, even if you only require small amounts. You can even get 1 book done, but the delivery fee to Singapore will be quite steep, costing you a total $29.99 + the actual book price of $3.25, so you can get your own book for only $33.24 USD.

The cheapest price you can get will be if you publish and ship 50 books, it will cost you $104.99 USD + $3.25 USD per book, which averages out to $6.95 SGD per book.

Note that the $3.25 USD is based on the member's direct price, which is the cost that you (as the book's author) incur to manufacture 1 book, with $0 royalty fee, of course. If you price at $29.90 on Amazon, you will get around $15 per book as royalty fee. Definitely good money, considering that from this point forth, it is all passive income.

CreateSpace also offers grammar, sentence structure and spelling check for a few hundred dollars, and cover design for another few hundred dollars. To find a really cheap way to publish, use the internal free Cover Creator and you can purchase some stock image for use as your front cover background (Note you might require extended license when you purchase the picture as you will be "re-selling" the image)

For the most updated information on pricing and royalty fees, check out www.createspace.com.

MAKING MONEY FROM YOUR BOOK

Every topic in this book is focused on building a marketing system to help you make money, and authoring your own book is no exception. Once your book is done, there are many ways to monetize it.

1) **Wait for the book to sell itself**

   You can just wait for the book to sell itself on the Amazon store, but more often than not, that is not likely to happen. Books usually only become best sellers after massive promotion campaigns, which will require having you or your publisher (If this is not yourself) coughing up the dough upfront.

2) **Bulk sale**

   If you are already doing paid speaking engagements, get the event organizer to purchase your books for distribution to the participants. You can even pay for it and give it out for free if you are sure they are your target audience, and you have a system to channel your readers to buy more products and services from you. It helps them retain whatever you spoke and also, they might pass your book to a friend if your seminar delivered real value. Who knows, that friend might be looking for a speaker on the topic you delivered, leading to even more bulk sales!

3) **Direct sale**

   You can use media to directly sell your book. You can even sell your book at a loss if you get your numbers right. Many authors do not make much money from the book, but the spin off from the externalities generated is astronomical.

   Let's say you sell 100 book, which actually costs you $10 per book to "sell" them. But you know that out of the 100 people who bought your books, 10 will engage you for a $500 project, and 1 will get a $2,000 project. So essentially you lost $1,000, but you still earned $3,500, based on a 50% margin, so your net profit is still $2,500.

   It is very possible to make a loss to sell your books, provided you have compelling content to position you as an expert in your industry, but you must have the system in place to capture all the leads, and turn them into paying customers.

   A few types of media you can use are Book Signing events, Facebook and LinkedIn advertising. As again, I would definitely recommend selling via online advertising, because it is much, much cheaper. Part IV explains in detail on how to use traffic platforms profitably.

4) **The Advance**

This is the amount that major publishers will give you after you sign a contract to write a book that they are going to publish when it is done. This can amount from $10,000 and up, however, it will take some time to find a publisher who is willing to give you an advance, especially if you are not that famous in the marketplace. If you have sufficient media credibility already, you can take a few months to find an established publisher who is willing to give you an advance, before you move on to the self-publishing route.

5) **Licensing**

You can license your brand to make T-shirts, motivational calendars, soft toys, greeting cards, puzzles, board games, conversation card, lunch boxes, journals, pet food for, more books, informational products and many more, limited only by your imagination.

As long as your brand image fits a certain product and resonates well with your readers, they will snap up the licensed products! For example if you sell a time management book, you can license your brand to promote a maximum productivity scheduler. The possibilities are limitless!

6) **Website Traffic**

People are more likely to visit your website if you have a book, and they just trust you more. People are also much more likely to buy if they have read your book before.

If your website is sales-optimized, meaning it will convert a good number of visitors into leads and then into paying customers, writing a book will become one of the most valuable thing you would have ever done.

7) **Additional Customers**

When people buy your book, you naturally get more customers, because you are the one who wrote the book.

You also get more referrals as it is an easy and low commitment way for people to refer you by simply passing others your book. Their friends can then judge for themselves if the book delivered value to them, and if they would like to further engage you.

8) Additional High Value Spinoff

Below is a long list of high value informational products you can create, which you can view as an extension of Point 5 above. I hope this can further expand your mind on what writing your first book can lead to, because the possibilities are simply amazing.

- Coaching Program
- Speaking Engagements
- Large scale Seminars
- Consulting projects
- Video training Series
- Membership sites
- Train-the-Trainer Programs
- Columns
- Trainings
- Boot camps
- Kits and Manuals
- Audio Programs
- Spinoff books
- Newsletters

9) Wide Open Doors

Having a book simply opens the door to many other opportunities, including invitations and introductions out of the blue you would never imagine you will get. You do not even need to sell the book. All you need is to write it, have the Amazon hyperlink on your website, and that's instant credibility. You can also pass every potential client a copy of your book for free when you meet up with them as a form of your own branding.

This also makes it easy for your client to help you to put the power of transferred trust to work. If you provide them with great value, they are likely to recommend you or your book and perhaps pass a copy of your book to them. And the next person who receives or purchases your book can possibly lead to a 5 figure training or consulting deal, and the opportunities lead to another, and another, all because your book is there to help push everything along.

10) Free Publicity

Having your own book also puts you on the map for being a celebrity, and it is much, much easier for people who are looking for guest speakers or interviews to put you on their radio or television programs and even magazines because you have a book to prove you are an subject matter expert. Even if your book does not sell like hotcakes immediately, do not worry, because it will surely pay for itself over time.

A lot of the ideas introduced in this book takes effort and time to accomplish, and you may not receive the benefits immediately. Patience and the ability to delay gratification are always found in highly successful people. Make this two values part of you and you will soon be among the ranks of these successful personalities.

Action Time!

*

Get started on writing your own book now! Go to www.createspace.com to create your own account and download a book template (I recommend 6 inch by 9 Inch) and write away! There is no need to organize your content. Just write the headings and then followed by the body! As you continue to write, the content page will become clear, and the title of the book will appear. Do not waste your time thinking of the perfect title, because it will keep changing over time, so don't bother in the first place!   ~

CHAPTER 10:

TRUST TOOL: VIDEOS

This is the cheapest and fastest way to build trust, as people can see you and they will start to feel like they know you even before they met you! Of course the drawback is that you will need to show up in the video for maximal trust building.

If you are shy about appearing on camera, perhaps this phrase will help: "Timid people have skinny kids". You will simply find it difficult to sell or do anything properly if you are not comfortable with communicating with others. Of course, there are alternative video formats, but still, these are issues you must resolve. I highly recommend you re-read Chapter 2 to overcome this inner game problem before you continue. You must absolutely believe that you are providing value, before you talk to other people about providing them value. Otherwise, you will find it tough to create great videos that genuinely helps other people, and hence, increasing their trust in you.

There are many different types of video, and let's cover a few types here and what they are best used for.

TYPES OF VIDEOS

The Read and Speak
This is a video in which a voiceover is provided for the sales script,

reading out the points that are flashed on the screen. It's best use is for summarizing points that have already been covered in detail.

It is also great as a sales video, either standalone or at the conclusion of a series, perhaps to summarize the benefits list.

The Talking Head

This is a video showing someone talking to you, the viewer. Usually, there are only 1 or 2 person in this kind of video. Due to the fact that there are live people talking, it helps to create trust, in the same way it would as someone talks to you more and more, and especially if what the person say makes sense and appeals to you. When the viewers know and trust the guys on the video, they will also trust what they recommend. You can also use this to spice up your 'About Us' page, a frequently viewed page for your site.

This type of video is great for introducing the premise of the video, asking for Calls to Action, giving Guarantees, and also for selling Coaching and Consulting programmes. As people watch your video, they will know more about what you are like, and will come to trust and feel that they know you well enough to start a Coaching or Consulting relationship with you.

Animation

This kind of videos is great for asking for opt-ins, because of its entertainment value. When asking for opt-ins, viewers generally are at the stage where they don't really know you yet, and so delivering value is a bit more difficult, because the trust is not really there. Hence, it relies on entertainment to capture attention, while delivering value to viewers, so that they are more likely to opt-in. This is also good for selling lower value products ($1-$100), as it can entertain and engage at the same time.

Camera Interview

Viewers get to listen in on an interview or conversation, usually between 2 person. This is great for Case Studies, Big Picture Concepts and Questions and Answers, because it is essentially a series of questions and answers, where the interviewer(s) will ask the common questions that many people have and you, as the consultant/expert can then answer the questions directly. This helps to explain concepts in a clearer form, and helps viewers to link all the concepts and ideas together into one coherent solution - Yours.

Virtual Interview

Similar to Camera Interviews, you can also do an online version, using platform such as Google Hangouts so that you can talk to people anywhere around the world.

This also helps you to create and sell affiliate products, where both product owners can meet up online to promote their products.

Screen Recording

So many of our society's current tasks depends on the computer, and learning how to perform these tasks are of great value to people who needs to learn and apply these technical knowledge. And the most efficient and effective way to learn this is via a well recorded and edited screen recording of someone performing the exact same tasks, and explaining the sequences of steps, as well as the nuances behind each step that is done.

These type of videos are great for such Training and Tutorial videos showing how to perform digital tasks. One other way to use this is for demonstrating proof elements of certain achievements, such as sales figures or number of visitors, due to the higher trust level and also the greater difficulty in creating such fraudulent videos.

Show and Tell

This type of videos are great for tutorial which requires setting up physical items and actual physical demonstrations for you to strut your stuff and position yourself to gain authority.

This is great for Training and Tutorials where real, physical items are involved, such as hands-on crafting, knitting or repairing items.

While there are different styles of videos, it does not mean that you should use each style exclusively for each video alone. In fact, it is best if you can mix the different styles around, so that each one best suits the message that you are trying to deliver.

DOING PRODUCT LAUNCHES

Product launches are a series of helpful videos that includes valuable content to help others solve their problem. Usually there are 3 to 4 videos, each with a duration of between 20-30 minute, spaced over a week, rather than combined into one long video. It could be a summary or involve demonstrating a small portion of the actual product. Usually the video training series is a lead-generation offer, so that you can learn about the product, so that you can subsequently decide if you want to buy the actual product at the end of the video training series. This is a powerful way to sell high priced products at between $2,000 to $4,000 dollars, and helps to keep the product fresh in the prospect's mind due to the anticipation that it creates.

Note that you will need to have around 1 hour of good content in total for selling information products, such as those on marketing, coaching and consulting at this price range.

COMMON VIDEO MISTAKES

Videos are great for creating trust, but if your video does not look good, people will not even watch it. Here are some simple mistakes you can easily learn and avoid to vastly improve the quality of the video you produce.

Copyright Issues

1. Video Footage - Make sure your videos don't include scenes from movies or other people's work. Purchase these licensed footages from sites like VideoHive.net. Cost ranges from $10 onwards.

2. Images - Make sure your photos are purchased or Royalty free. Use sites like gettyimages.com, Fotolia.com or iStock Photo. Google 'free stock images' to find more sites.

3. Music - Make sure all of your music is licensed or royalty free. Purchase licensed music from places like AudioJungle.net. It only costs below $25 per track, and the variety is simply amazing.

Teleprompter Mistakes

1. Not aligning the prompter and the text "read lines" directly to the camera causing the eye line to not "look" at the viewer" when talking

2. Keeping the prompter too close or the fonts too small, causing your eyes to go back and forth (The viewer will know that you are reading off a screen!)

3. Having the text scroll too fast or too slow making you sound tired or rushed instead of natural

4. Trying to read the voiceover and operate the PowerPoint or Keynote presentation at the same time

Lighting Mistakes

1. Not enough light on the subject. A properly exposed person (Face) is ALL that matters.

2. Mixing Color Temperatures of Lights. Rule of Thumb - Hot Lights are orange, LEDs are Blue/Green, Florescent are Green.

3. Make sure that you can see a glint of light (One or two, not 4, 5, 6,etc.) in the talents eyes.

4. For Presentation Video, light it "Flat", meaning even light across the subject. Don't go for drama unless you're... going for drama.

5. Position your lights at the height of the top of your subjects head or above.

6. Put an Edge Light on a Subject to help separate them from the background. An Edge Light is a light that is behind the subject lighting their shoulders and head.

Presentation Mistakes

1. Asking someone who has never read from a Teleprompter before to do so.

2. Not rehearsing your lines. If you want to sound dull and wooden, then absolutely don't rehearse. Only rehearse if you want excellent results.

3. Big, fat pauses before you start speaking and after you finish. Edit out dead air.

4. Shaky-cam filming. It can be an art form but it causes nausea most of the time because it's done badly. Avoid this as much as possible by making sure you use a tripod.

5. When you blow a line when reading a voice over, do the entire line over. Fragments of lines makes voice editing really tough, especially the part where you think you should pick up. It's easier to just start the sentence over.

6. MOVE! Try to have as much movement in the video as possible. Movement resets the viewers' attention span, and keeps them watching your video longer. The longer they watch, the more value they get, and the more likely they will buy. So keep them watching!

7. Don't put things in there just to be cool. If it does not fit in with the message then don't add it. Your message need to be as long as it needs to be to get your ideal message across and not one second longer or shorter.

8. Not doing the scripting first. You should let the SCRIPT create your ideas for locations and "Skits" and not the other way around. Once you have a good script copy, then ideas for locations, skits, small gags will come. You want to get your message across while being entertaining and not the other way around.

9. Writing a Voice Over or Video Script that sounds like it was meant to be read, not spoken. Make all of your scripts sound conversational and not formal, no matter what the topic.

10. Over-stuffing your slides with bullet points and/or excessive text.

11. Inappropriate hand placement: Your hands should be relaxed and by your side with one hand in a fist in between the first and second knuckle of the same hand, or you can join hands by holding the left thumb with your right fist. Practice this.

12. Don't forget to acknowledge the other person when there are 2 of you on camera. 50% of acting is knowing how to "listen" (and react) when another person is talking. Make sure to continue to look back and forth between the camera (viewer) and the person talking. Nod, chuckle and make the appropriate faces or reactions when the time is right to keep the viewer engaged to both people.

Style Mistakes

1. The reason why people like to watch videos is because of the movement. As long as there is movement on the screen, then people are more likely to keep watching. One great comparison I have seen is 2 videos, which are using the same presentation slides, and voice over. The difference is that one is animated, while the other is not. Movements such as when the words become typed in then fade out, appear and then dissolve then swings in and drops out will make for a much more eye grabbing video sales letter and presentation than having all the contents in the slide appear at once. The finish rate of the animated slides is over 50% more than the other!

2. Pacing and Tempo is 75% of keeping a viewer glued to the screen. Don't give 10 minutes of on-camera talking and expect anyone to be left at the end of the video. Break it up with different shots, angles and use different media formats (Slides, Screen Captures, Animations, Titles, Locations, etc.)

3. Boring Video - GET OUTSIDE of YOUR Comfort zone. Be daring. Kick Ass. Be bold and viewers will stay   glued to your videos. Make a Joke. Express Emotion. Be Angry, Sad, Passionate.... Be a PERSON. Remember that you are now in the INFO-TAINMENT Business. Teach and Tickle.

4. Wrong video style - Use the right style for the right type of landing page. Doodle videos are best for Opt-in pages or Webinar registrations, while things like white board videos are best for teaching and communication for customers, JV Partners and affiliates.

5. Being Gender Specific - If your script has a lot of "Him, He, Man, Boy" and the topic is not gender specific, add some "Her, She, Woman, Girl"

6. Vocals that lacks emotion - Vary your vocal inflections to create emphasis. Just like a bold, underline, or italic creates attention, so should your vocal performance.

7. Swearing - If you're going to swear, make sure it's for a damn good reason, because if you do it just a little too much, they leave...

Message Mistakes

1. Story Structure - Not creating a logical flow of story. Start with The Problem, moving on to explain the STORY that lead you to discover the solution, describe why your solution works. The general flow is like this: Describe your first attempt at using the solution, the improvements you made to your solution, the outcome and the improvement the viewer will experience once they have successfully used the product.

2. Poor Use of Benefits (Feature Loading) - Don't just list the features of a product without telling what the feature does. e.g. Don't JUST list the feature: "It will help you to understand the product more", make sure to explain the benefit like "It helps you to understand the product more, so that you can convince your

customers better and sell a lot faster and easier." You can even go a step further and explain the benefits of the benefit: "It helps you to understand the product more, so that you can convince your customers better and sell a lot faster and easier and achieve the dream career and lifestyle that you want"

3. Not using a Cold Open – You should hook your viewer immediately with a promise of the value of the video they're about to watch before doing fancy logos or musical opens.

4. Get Response - Remember I said before not to be a professional visitor. Get your viewers to do something! Some videos have weak or even no Call-to-Action! Don't be afraid to tell the viewer what to do next. Don't wimp out here. Tell the viewer what to do. "Click the add to cart button", or "enter your name and email", etc. If you want a comment, ask for it. Want a like or share, ASK for it.

5. Not linking the ideas together - Just because you can clearly see and understand your "Breakthrough" idea does not mean that your viewers can – explain it in detail for them. Don't assume that the final outcome is understood by the viewer. Make it plain - Good, Bad, Amazing, Terrible, Life Altering, etc. Draw conclusions for your viewers!

Audio Mistakes

1. Letting words like "Uh..." or "Uhm" remain in your finished product. Edit them out. Lower the volume to silence on those phrases when you're on camera so you don't need to create a visual edit.

2. Over-modulated audio (Intense signal, causing audio levels to be in the "red".) or inconsistent audio levels – Some audio tracks are louder while others are softer as they are recorded in different places using different equipment. You will need to us the "NORMALIZE" function in your audio editor to smooth out different audio levels.

3. No Noise Reduction on Voice Tracks - All audio recordings will need some form of noise removal. If you use Camtasia, its internal noise remover will suffice. Free alternatives such as Audacity can do the job as well, under the "Effects" tab, choose the "Noise Removal" function.

Microphone Mistakes

1. Putting a Lapel or Lavaliere Microphone in a place where it's going to get jostled or rub against clothing

2. Microphones placed too far away - This will cause unnecessary background noise to be recorded, and post production sound editing will be more tedious.
   For Desktop microphones, you want to be within 12 inches of the pick-up

3. Having your Lapel or Lavaliere Microphone too close or too far away from your mouth. With your chin at your chest, the mic should be about 2 inches from it in normal environments - closer in noisy places

4. Plosives - "Popping" sound caused by saying words with the letter "P" directly into a mic where there is no "pop" filter.

5. Using too many microphones - Mixing too many different microphones creates inconsistent sound. Try to limit to one "On Camera" Mic and one "Screen Capture" or "Presentation" mic.

6. Not having a windscreen on your mic when shooting outside

Video Camera Mistakes

1. Not enough light - A $500 camera shoots better video than a $5,000 camera if it has enough light. Shoot and experiment before you invest in expensive equipment.

2. Using digital zoom - This degrades resolution. You can use either optical (Lens) zoom or you can move the camera closer

3. Wrong camera height - The Camera should be at the subject's eye level unless you're doing something tricky

4. Not shooting with a tripod - Unless you have a specific motivation to shoot handheld, lock your camera down.

5. Not white balancing the camera - Do it every time you change location. DON'T USE AUTO WHITE BALANCE especially if you change location frequently.

6. Shooting a subject with the sun or other bright light behind them - Could cause lens flares which make your video washed out in certain parts of the frame

7. Avoid shooting High Frame Rates like 60p, unless you need to. (E.g. For hardcore sports demonstration or slow-motion) Stick with 30p or 24p. Also avoid Interlaced video formats, as they cause artifacts on most screens

8. Too much or not enough headroom when shooting a person. Learn about the "Rule of Thirds" for camera composition and framing

9. Using the wrong focal length. When photographing a person, longer lens are better - i.e. Move the camera away from the subject and zoom in about 50% of the lens length to get the best "portrait" look.

10. Focus the lens so that the pupils of the eyes are in the most focus.

Location & Setting Mistakes

1. Including Bogies and other distractions - Look for and avoid "Bogies" (Stray objects such as People, Cords, Blinking lights, animals, etc) in the frame. Also avoid distracting decorations, furniture, excessively bright TV screens or computer monitors in the shot. Simple and elegant is better, especially for web videos

2. View obstruction – Place the subject where nothing intersects their head (Tree, door frame, window frame, light stand, etc are all distracting and should be avoided)

3. Noisy location - Even in your home, your refrigerator or dishwasher is enough to pollute your audio signal. Watch out for the hum of florescent lights. Bring Headphones to monitor your audio signal

4. Not Enough Power - Think your camera battery is all you need? What if the shoot runs long? What if the batteries in your wireless run out?

5. Not bringing extension cords - Buy a bunch in the 10 to 20 meters range. Get green or black so they don't pop out in camera if they're accidentally seen.

6. Shooting on Private Property without permission or public property without a permit.

7. Shooting and including logos, storefronts and/or identifiable businesses without permission.

Visual Mistakes

1. No additional lighting - If you're inside, you need lights

2. Lacking continuity - Wear the same shirt or outfit from scene to scene. Hair Up? Hair Down? Using your right hand to give someone something in one take and left hand in another?

3. NOT zooming in - When screen-casting (recording what you are doing on screen), you should zoom in to show areas of interest or detail. It strains your viewers' eye to decipher the details, so zoom in to make your video more enjoyable.

4. Having a cluttered desktop. (Files, Programs, etc.) Hide everything. There are simple shortcuts for both Mac and PC, so use it and remove the clutter.

5. Not using your desktop image as a branding opportunity

6. Making viewers wait - Entering URLs, waiting for web page loads, or making typos when filling out forms are all time wasters and should be edited off.

7. Making everything flat and static - Use as much angles and movements on your videos as you can to keep your audience engaged. Every time there is movement on the screen, the audience's attention span is reset, which keeps them watching the videos longer.

8. Wrong Aspect Ratio - Using a PowerPoint slide that is square in a widescreen video

9. Inconsistent Eye-lines - Always pick a spot to look at when you're on camera and keep your eyes there.

Technical and Encoding Mistakes

1. Mixing different frame rates. I.e. Shooting at 29.97, screen capturing at 30p. Editing in a 23.98 timeline. Audio will drift out of sync in this example

2. Not making a back-up of your media. Always, Always, Always back-up your stuff. Use cloud storage backup in case your workstation goes down to fire, flood, or other disasters.

3. Trying to do a Green Screen Key without enough light on the Green Screen. Oh, also - don't move the camera unless you know how to do motion tracking

4. Starting your videos with complex and dynamic imagery. Start with simple images so the encoding stream is small and rapidly buffers into your viewer's player

5. Not test recording to ensure all the connections and configurations of your camera, microphone, software, etc. are correct and getting signal

6. Assuming that if you don't have a "Mac", that you can't do video. I spend most of my time on a Windows laptop doing video. All of the programs that I use except 2 (Keynote and Screenflow) are on both a mac and a PC

7. Encoding in a Frame Rate that is not the same source as your media. If you shoot at 30p, encode your final file at 30p

8. Not encoding for Mobile (i.e avoid Flash video)

9. Only encoding for Web - Make a High Quality Master (It will be a HUGE FILE) as a master back up. You will likely re-use this as a template in the future

10. Encoding your audio with too much bandwidth. If you're only speaking, set your channel output to Mono and set the bit rate to 60kb at 32Khz.

.

CHAPTER 11:

TRUST TOOL – WEBSITE & BLOG

Before you start getting or purchasing traffic, you should look into the design and integration for your website. Is your website doing what it's supposed to be doing? As mentioned at the start of the book, I would assume all readers want to generate a profit for themselves and their businesses. And to convert visitors into paying customers, following up is the key. And if you have not heard it before, remember this: "Email is King"

Many, many people have become millionaires, just by sitting at home, creating multiple email lists to promote and sell other people's online products. They did not even create their own products to sell! This is also known as affiliate marketing, which requires a slightly different approach, as your traffic sources must be cheaper than if you are selling your own products.

Hence, you will definitely need email auto-responder integration on your website to capture information from people, especially their emails, so that you can follow up with them cheaply. I will elaborate further in Chapter 12.

BUILDING A WEBSITE

How much do you think a website costs these days? It surprises people, but it really only cost less than $200 to start and maintain a website for a year. At this price, nobody should go without a website. If you are an employee, this will get you hired at a premium. If you are in sales, you save a lot of time convincing people about your competency and authenticity. If you own a small business, it is the key to bringing sales to the next level. There are lots of information on the internet which shows you how to get your website started. The best way is to set up a self-hosted Wordpress website on a shared hosting server. This is the cheapest and yet gives you the full functionality and flexibility of a complete website when you need to add more features later on.

However, if you still prefer to get help, I can help you to get it done up for only a charge of $30. By the time you read this, the price might have changed, but I promise you it will still be affordable! Get more information at www.rmvic.com.

When you are just getting started, I do not recommend hiring a designer do up a fancy website. Just get a basic one with the functionalities you need done up and then improve along the way. There is no point at all in having a nice website, when it does not serve its purposes. Nowadays, even basic websites look presentable, and are flexible enough that you can always make changes as and when you require any extra features.

Once you are making a good profit, then you can afford to splurge a bit more on revamping your website to make it look more fanciful.

THE PURPOSE OF YOUR SITE

For Visitors

You must know the primary reasons why visitors come to your site. Do they want more information on a certain thing? Or are they looking to purchase products and services from you?

Arrange your website in a way that it helps them to quickly achieve their objectives. Let them know that you know what they want, and show them how you can help them solve their problem.

Ensure that it is clear what your visitors' next steps are; give clear directions on what you want them to do, instead of requiring them to search high and low for it.

For you, the Business Owner

Obviously, a website is very effective on providing information to your prospective customers about your product and services.

However, there is one other very important reason for owning your blog or website: TO GET THEIR CONTACT DETAILS. If you do not give them something to take away to read, they'll likely never come back. That's why you not only give them an instant download to read through, but also capture their emails, so that you can continue to send them useful information for them to remember you. Only when you have a list, can you have a flow of leads whom you can slowly nurture to become paying customers. Better yet if you can give your customers a reason to give you their phone number.

The list type may be different, but there are few industries where you can't build customer lists. Even emergency services can get people to sign up to inform the medical institutions of their prior medical conditions first, or they can offer preferred rates for patients who have signed up in advance.

THE PURPOSE OF YOUR HOMEPAGE

You need to communicate the brand / USP and convert people into subscriber. It is a landing page to get your potential customers to do something, and not a page to show your latest post.

What immediately catches your eye when you reach your home page? Ideally, it should be your opt-in box or bribe with the picture displayed conspicuously. The below 2 are also problems, and you should also rectify it.

1) Something other than your primary purpose catches your eye
2) Nothing catches your eye

SEPARATE LANDING PAGES

If you are doing paid advertisement, it will be good to have a different landing page for every advertisement set that you have. Have it customized to solve the exact problems that the customer group have, rather than have a one size fits all landing page.

For example, let's say you help your clients to generate more sales online. Break the problem down into different components of the same problem, such as:

1) Small List Number
2) Low Traffic
3) Low Conversion
4) Poor Follow Up

Then have different landing pages for each component of the problem. This will allow you to tell a more specific message about what your clients want, which will definitely increase the conversion rate.

You can also do this from another angle: Different problems that the same product or service can solve. For example, female weight solutions solves problem from different perspective.

1) Prevents husband's or boyfriend's eye from straying
2) Class reunion in a month time
3) Purely for health reasons

As again, having different landing pages for each benefit of the benefit will cause a spike in your conversion rate.

If you are just starting out, this might be too much work so a single landing page is fine. You can always improve it at a later stage, when you have more resources to optimize your conversion rate. Note however, if your conversion rate is not giving you a positive ROI over a 1 week period, then you definitely have to adjust either your landing page, offer or angle. Hoping that the conversion rates will change by itself is naïve; it's much easier to take responsibility to change, refine and resume.

THE F PATTERN

This is a frequent pattern which appears on website click maps, which shows that people clicks in a F shaped pattern on your website, no matter if it is a home page or other pages. The takeaway point from the F pattern is that

1) It creates rest points for the eye to rest on, at every starting and ending point of the strokes on the letter F and you should put important components at these rest points, such as an opt-in box or download.

2) If you want people to click the ads, you can also place them at

the rest points or on the F pattern itself.

RESOURCES PAGE

This is an excellent page that you can create, because it is an easy way for people to keep coming back, especially if it is frequently updated with the latest information, tips and tricks that you know your viewers will be interested in.

Theme your blog posts and group them into specific guides on how to do a certain thing. It sort of works like categorizing, but then it's like you are selecting the best of the best so on a smaller and more specific topic, rather than a general concept. For example, a general concept you might use for your Category would be how to set up a website or blog to sell your products and services, while on this resource page, you can re-organize a few posts into "The best payment gateway for a membership site"

LEARNING WHAT YOUR AUDIENCES WANT

As you start building an audience, you will definitely have some ideas of what to talk about. But over time, as the environment changes, your audience will want to know about different things, or perhaps certain specific things in detail. Don't wait for them to ask you. Be proactive and find out what your readers want:

1. Watching comments
2. Ask-the-Readers Posts
3. Running Surveys
4. Social Media
5. Question and Answer Calls
6. Webinars
7. Emails to your list. You can build questions into your auto responder sequence so you get a consistent flow of questions or content ideas.

Generally you will want to find out and answer these 3 problems that your readers have.

1. What are they struggling on right now?

2. What are their biggest frustrations about?
3. How can you help?

Going a step further, asking yourself and your customers these questions help you to create your product with your customer groups in mind.

1. What free thing would you like to receive from me?
2. What products have you considered buying in the last few or next few months?
3. What product are you looking to buy if someone is smart enough to make it for you?

It is best to have a 2 way conversation to involve your audience. Go back and ask them if you understood them correctly. When they are involved in the product creation process, they are invested and they are much more inclined to buy it

ARTICLES / POSTS WITH HYPNOTIC HEADLINES

This is a simple thing, but because of its simplicity, people might actually miss it out. A good head line catches reader's attention, helps them to remember what you want to say, and keeps the reader coming back, sometimes to review and recap the same thing that they have already seen.

SOCIAL PROOF AND SOCIAL MEDIA BUTTONS

Some business owners make the mistake of including too many social media buttons. You probably want Facebook, Google and Twitter. However, beyond these common few, you really have to decide what other platforms your readers are using, whether it is Instagram, Pinterest or any other platforms.

People tend to follow the crowd and if you demonstrate signs of social approval, then new visitors will find it easier to trust you as well.

Here's a Social Proof List to give you some ideas:

- Testimonials
- Comments

- Emails
- Surveys
- Tweets
- Facebook posts
- LinkedIn Recommendations
- Follower Counts RSS counts
- Places you have guest posted, been interviewed or published
- Be on the lookout for other sources as well
- Keep these materials in Evernote, so that you can remember what social proof you have received, so that you may use or post them in the future.

OPTIMIZING THE OPT-IN FUNNEL

The opt in funnel refers to the entire process of your web visitor seeing your opt-in box, with its opt in bribe, all the way to them actually receiving your email in your inbox. There are various steps involved, and following the below recommendations will help you to build your visitor list faster, with lesser effort.

1) Opt-In form
   Below are a few prominent places where you can and should place your opt-in form. This is the primary reason of your website, so try to make this ever present, so that when they eventually want to join your email list, they can do so quickly, without having to look for it. It is also good to have a sign-up form at the end of every blog post, so that every reader knows and are repeatedly asked to opt-in or subscribe.
   You must also offer an opt-in bribe for your visitors so that they want to join your list. Usually a visually appealing cover page of the download will suffice, but you can always offer more, like a trial or a video series to further increase the sign up rate.

   Website integration with all of the other traffic sources is vital so that you can test and improve your conversion ratio.

   a) Top, above the fold

b) Top of sidebar
c) Directly below content
d) In-content "Stop Points"
e) Footer
f) Slide-up, Pop-up lightbox,
Your home page will definitely need to have a bottom slide up as a pop up as it is non-intrusive, yet offer an excellent way for people to join your list.
g) Exit redirect
Exit re-direct is also a vital part of the website design, as it usually retains a 20% of the leaving traffic on your mailing list.

2) Confirmation Page
Ask them to confirm email immediately. Provide a direct link for them to click to their email, so that can confirm the email on the spot.

3) Confirmation Email
Don't include too much information here, because all you really want is for them to click the link to confirm. Further information can always be sent later, via your auto responder series.

4) Thank you page
Stand out by using unique, funny, or creative language and graphics, or maybe even include a short Thank You video to this page. You already know that your subscribers want to know more, so this is a great time to seize their enthusiasm.
Invite them to follow you on Twitter or Facebook, subscribe to your blog, or learn more about your product or service via content links. It's also a good time to ask them to refer their friends.

5) Welcome Email
As soon as someone registers, your email marketing software should immediately send them a welcome email, which usually contains:
• Thank you!
• Congratulations, you now on our mailing list!

- Here is your offer (fulfill the promise of the opt-in by sending the coupon code, content, or other promised offer).
- Here is what to expect next how often you'll email, and when to expect it.
- Leave open loops so that they want to anticipate your future emails. Always have open loops for you readers to think about your future emails.
- You can also include some ideas discussed in point 4) above.

VALUE PER VISITOR

This is the a very important number when you are determining how much you can pay for your web traffic. How many visitors are seeing your website, and how many are actually signing up for whatever that you are offering?

You do not need the exact figures, because it can take a lot of time to set it up, but you will need to be 80% correct when you are just starting out.

Let's say you do Facebook advertisement for $30 a day, and you get around 3 leads on average, and 1 turns into a trial customer who pays you $50. This will definitely make for a profitable campaign. You might even want to scale it up if the increase in the number of leads is proportional to the increase in spending amount.

At the end of the day, this reduces the multidimensional percentages into dollars and cents: How much advertisement dollars you put in vs how much sales you get out of it.

The problem with percentages is that it usually does not tell the full story. High CTR does not mean high actual sales, because the quality of the visitors might have dropped. High sales number might not mean higher revenue, if customers bought the cheaper product.

Hence, the best way is to track exactly how much revenue did the advertisement generate. It might seem like a complex process, but the tool at www.hypertracker.com works great. It merely places a tracking code at the entry page, and a unique Thank You page (Perhaps for when the visitor bought something or when they subscribed to a newsletter). It then shows you at one glance how many people visited the page, how many of them took action and whether the campaign is making you money, or if it's just a loss maker.

In other words, you get a complete picture of what your paid for vs what you receive in return.

CHAPTER 12:

USING AUTO RESPONDERS

If you want a long term business, you have to implant this idea of "Making a sale to get a customer" into your subconscious mind. Not "Getting a customer to make the sale"; it is much more difficult to achieve wealth and freedom this way. Selling to a new customer is always more expensive, remember?

So how are you supposed to maintain constant contact with your customers? Social media can be good, but there is really no better way than using email Auto Responders that sends out automatic emails on your behalf.

You might say, "Oh, I don't want to be sending spam mails to other people". But the truth is, if you actually provide value to other people, they will WANT to receive updates from you!

But note, the key is that your content must be useful or engaging, so that your customers will not mind receiving your email in their inbox.

AWeber and GetResponse are both highly rated pay-as-you-use auto responders that have high delivery rates, excellent customer service and great ease of use.

AWeber will cost $19 USD a month for up to 500 subscribers, with a quarterly and annual payment option, which will save you around 15% off the base rate. The next price step will cost additional $10 per month for up to 2,500 subscribers, costing you $29 a month

GetResponse starts at $15 USD for 1,000 subscribers and $25 for up to 2,500 subscribers, with an 18% discount on the entire amount if you make annual payment up front. For every price step, GetResponse is slightly cheaper, and if you would to get started on a simple, easy-to-build auto responder service, I would recommend GetResponse

However, for more advanced marketers who wants affordable list segmentation option or marketers who want more control in the future, AWeber has a third party service called AWProTool. It costs an additional $29.99 USD per month on top of the normal AWeber price of $19 USD. This allows for dynamic segmentation of the market. For example, if your website is about increasing sales online, you can break into 4 different aspects, like what you can do for different landing pages, which are:

1. Small list number
2. Low traffic
3. Low conversion
4. Bad follow up

You can then send a different free video or report to each of this subgroup, and AWProTool will automatically tag them to be within a certain subgroup. This subgroup will automatically receive another designated set of emails with information and promotions related to whichever topic they expressed interest in, greatly increasing message to market match.

This is excellent for those who wants more control at a reasonable price, but there is definitely more work involved because you need to set up the different "email paths" that the customer can take.

Normally internet marketers would think that sending a frequent email, each around 3 days apart with good quality information for more than a year will be enough to stay at the top of mind of the customer. This will translate to 120 emails per year

If you require 4 additional path ways, and let's say each path is 5 emails (usually 1 – 2 days apart), this will be an additional 20 emails for a year.

More advanced email automation software includes Ontraport, Infusionsoft and Marketo in increasing price steps and lots of bells and whistles of course. Depending on the stage of business you are in, it might be worthwhile to set it up.

THE FOLLOW UP EMAIL

Do not make the mistake that just because email is free, everyone would want to get on your email list. Because it's not totally free – It costs your prospect's time to key in their contact information and also the time to read whatever you send them in your emails.

And if you don't help your subscribers save time, then they will leave you. Here are a few other ways you can use to grow your customer base.

1. Via QR code or your Facebook page.
2. Using old-school paper advertising techniques.
3. During presentations such as tradeshows and conferences (Have a tablet on hand to easily opt-in new contacts)
4. In the middle of an e-commerce checkout or during an actual in-store checkout.
5. Through a prompt at the end of a survey
6. Via online whitepaper/eBook/ webinar online registration
7. With a suggested opt-in prompt on a paper receipt or invoice.
8. When an existing subscriber shares your email in any social media and one of their friends opts-in to your list.
9. On physical banner advertisements. Yes, those big cloth banners you see along walkways.

CREATING ENGAGING CONTENT

"The best marketing doesn't feel like marketing at all"

Everybody says this, but what does it mean? It basically means that you can enjoy some of the benefits of a trusted relationship by marketing to the buyer in a natural, non-marketing way that creates value for their readers.

And what gives value to the reader really depends the culture and industry that your business is in. Sometimes it might be ok for to send out daily updates, like some news websites that helps reporters get articles to write about. Other times, a once-a-week industry news update is the most that you can send out in more stable or slower moving industries.

It would be helpful if you can remember what I call The Subscriber Pledge:

Dear Subscriber,
We promise to:
- Send emails that you enjoy and want.
- Deliver only those emails with value to you.
- Consolidate information to send you the most targeted and relevant information.

Yours Sincerely,
The Helpful Marketer

Keeping this pledge in mind will be your Back-to-Basics motto about how you can create engaging content your subscribers would be excited to hear about.

CONSISTENCY

1. Keep types of content consistent. If you usually send a teaser email as a precursor to a full blog post on your website, then keep it that way. It helps your customer to know what to expect.
2. Brand consistently. Your emails should usually look similar.
3. Use the same name and reply to email addresses. Your emails should "look" similar when they hit a recipient's inbox.
4. There are also advocates who recommends sending emails at the same times, on the same days of the week and even maintain sending the same number of emails every month.
   It can probably bump up a couple percentage points. But unless you are spending upwards of $5,000 a month on marketing, this probably does not make a significant difference for most businesses. Yes, it does create the right expectations, but I do not think that most of your readers would notice such detail. I see a lot of my readers wait till they have a series of emails before read all of it at the same time.

ALWAYS RELEVANT

Relevance comes in 2 components, and that you need to say the right things (Correct Message Content) to the right people (Using Behavioral Segmentation). I elaborate more below:

1. Talk to the right people.
You must know who your audience is and what they want from your emails. You want your subscribers to think, "You know who I am. You know what I want. You get me". If you aren't relevant, your subscribers will opt-out or worse, emotionally opt-out.
Segmenting and targeting customers by using an email marketing solution is the best way to send the right message to your subscribers.

Let's take my Business Consultancy as an example. Most of my clients can be divided into 2 general groups: Upcoming Entrepreneurs and Current Business owners.

If I send content that talks about recruitment and HR management strategies, it would not interest the Upcoming Entrepreneur, who is currently running a 1 man business.
Similarly, if I send content that talks about the nitty-gritty procedures of setting up a company, it is totally irrelevant to a business owner who has already set up his first business.

Of course, further segmentation is possible, and it will really depend on your current revenue and profit margins to justify the additional cost that comes with increased segmentation

2. Say the right things.
Put thought into your content or call on a talented team to write and design your emails. A few points that you can use to say the right things.

5 Ways to Be More Human in Your Email Marketing Message
1. Ditch the dull corporate and jargon filled lingo
2. Add humor.
3. Include customer stories.
4. Weave in real-world events and pop culture.

5. Don't take yourself too seriously!

There are only 4 main reasons why you should be mailing your subscribers. Does every mail perform well in at least one of the below aspects?
1. Solve her problem
2. Save her money
3. Make her smarter
4. Entertain her

And below are 5 effective subject line categories you can use:
1. Educate: "7 things content marketers can learn from fiction writers."
2. Ask a question: "Did you miss this?"
3. Announce a sale or new product: "Save up to 50%: Our semi-annual sale starts today."
4. Offer a solution to a problem: "Pay down your loan. Here's how"
5. Jump on a popular topic: "The state of the Facebook Newsfeed: What's working now?"

Here's an example of email subject line sequence that tries to make the follow up as conversational as possible. Is yours similar?

- Welcome! Here's what to expect.
- Check out this article.
- Here's a useful video.
- Happy birthday!
- See our latest product.
- Share this with friends.
- What others like.
- Download our new book.
- Are you ready to buy?
- More great content for you!
- Want to join us at our event?
- You've seen X, you'll probably like Y too!
- Fun ways to learn more about our products (or services)!
- Take this survey?
- You haven't bought X yet, so here's a 20% discount.

CONSTANT IMPROVEMENT

To stay ahead of the game, optimize and test to learn what works and what doesn't. But take note, test and improve only when you have a stable working model, generating a constant source of revenue.

If not, keep implementing new things, so that you have 80% of all the components and systems set up and running. Only after you have a presence on all the platforms, then you can begin on the next 20%. Start with the component that generates you the most revenue, using the Recency, Frequency, Monetary value (RFM) model to decide which component that is the most valuable to start with.

PART IV: TRAFFIC

The money is wherever people are at.

Even if you have the best product, with the perfect message, sure to drive people into a buying frenzy, you still would not be able to sell anything if nobody knows it exist.

This is a part of the Economics equation as well, as the cost of reaching out to customers must give you sufficient margin to cover all other costs and still leave you a profit. Anybody can sell anything if they have enough cash to burn to fuel the flames of Marketing. But the trick is to be able to do it profitably, taking care not to let it run out of control, or it will burn a serious hole in your pocket, or worse, cause the whole company to collapse.

The trick is to start with the cheapest form of paid advertising, which is currently Facebook, followed by LinkedIn, then followed by Google. This is based on my experience of extensive usage of online advertising, and you can test it cheaply for yourself. Using this 3 pillars of marketing well is enough to jumpstart ANY business.

Note that you must absolutely follow the set-up in Part III to profitably and CONSISTENTLY get customers over a 2 month period before you start tweaking with the rules. Better stick with the rules, until you get a better sense of the market place, than to pay what Internet Marketers call "Stupidity Tax". This happens if you do not optimize your marketing system and platform variables, such as keywords, demographics, interests and positions, leading to excessive and unnecessary marketing costs.

Chapter 6 and 7 of Part III can be considered the front end of Marketing System, which gets people to respond, while the rest of the chapters in Part III helps your customers come to the conclusion that working with you will definitely be useful and valuable to them. The entire Part III should work in harmony, so that your advertising time (Networking) and dollars (Paid Advertisement) are well spent.

MULTIPLE TRAFFIC SOURCES FOR MAXIMUM TRUST

In order to build awareness and trust, a complex multi-media, multi-step marketing campaigns will work best.

Here are 2 examples

1. Online – Offline –Online
    You can get lots of cheap, yet high quality, online traffic through the various methods that I will introduce in the following chapters. From there, you can get their personal particulars to send them more useful information such as books or promotions via direct mail, and of those who do not buy, you can continue to follow up with them using email.

2. Offline – Online – Offline
    Offline drive works best when you can offer a low cost, but useful gift or voucher in exchange for getting customers to sign up as members so you can continue to market to them. Then you can send direct mail to further follow up.

Having a fixed sequence where your customers can go through is the key to maximizing your Total Customer Value. An example of a fixed sequence is when you have multiple products, arranged as upsells or downsells, as the next step when people buy or don't buy. You can also include pure information pieces to build trust before asking them to buy in the next message. The point here is that you need to have your "What's next" planned and communicated to your customers, so that they never get bored.

ONLINE VS OFFLINE ADVERTISING

There are many more traffic sources that you can purchase offline than online. You simply call up any ad agency, purchase perhaps a few pages on a magazine, do up some designs and then you pay a fixed amount. However, the difficult part to control is that you do not know if it is going to be profitable or not. And that's the reason this book is focused solely on online advertisement methods. Once you can make money online, then you can slowly expand your reach to more expensive media platforms. It is much cheaper to acquire a customer online than offline due to the unparalleled connective power of the internet, and also because of its almost real time feature (Perhaps 15 minutes delay before your modified ad shows up), you can quickly make adjustments to your advertisements in order to make it profitable. Gone are the days when you have to sink in thousands of dollars just to find out if the advertisement worked, because most business don't have this kind of money to toy with.

Most businesses need to know if the method works or not, because they need to cut their losses early.

CONVERSION COUNTS MORE

I just would like to re-emphasize that the reason why the 5 parts of this book is ordered in this manner is that the message is more important than the where you get the traffic.

It's easy to purchase traffic and show people your message, but there really isn't any point if they do not
1) Click through and visit your site AND
2) Leave their contact information so that you actually get a lead

Hence the advertisement message and the picture, or the creative part of both advertisements and landing pages is very, very important for the marketing system to be profitable. Please refer back to Part II to recap on how to create a compelling message.

CHAPTER 13:

GOOGLE

This topic can fill up an entire book by itself, so I will just focus on a few key pointers that shows results really quick.

You might be surprised that Google in fact costs more among than LinkedIn and Facebook, but it's true, because there are a lot of impulsive clickers out there who will waste your marketing dollars quickly, without a second thought, especially if your website does not convert well. Or you might have the wrong types of keywords in the first place.

Google Adwords is for inbound advertising, and while it is good for people who knows what they are looking for, it also means you cannot present yourself to others who do not know that they need your product, which can limit your reach and traffic source. There are only so many people searching for your products and services right now, and the clicks might not be worth it because people like to price shop on Google.

While LinkedIn clicks is not much cheaper, but it does allow you to reach out to a highly targeted population, so it is not so limited in terms of traffic. The people there are not as likely to price shop, especially if you offer them good information and good value at the outset.

Facebook clicks are currently the cheapest amongst the 3, perhaps because it is still new. However don't expect it to stay that way forever, because online advertising can change a the snap of a finger. If used properly, Facebook is the most powerful platform for B2C selling. It is more difficult to use for B2B selling though.

Google Display Network is a much less competitive arena, however, because it requires that much more finesse to maneuver. As with all forms of medium, it can be profitable if you use it correctly.

GOOGLE PLACES FOR LOCAL BUSINESS

This is a really easy way to get your business found, really easy to set up as well and it's free! All you need is a Google account to set up your page, with all your business's operations and information.
It does take 2 weeks for you to receive the Google mailer at your business address for verifying your business, so get your Google Page done right after you get your business address.

KEYWORD RESEARCH

This is the critical part that people do not spend enough time on before starting the Adwords campaign.
Fully understand how the Google Keywords research tool works, before you continue. Additional tools you can use is wordtracker.com and longtailpro.com.

MATCH TYPE

Broad match (No symbol required)
This means just typing in keywords or keyphrases without any delimiters. For example, your keyphrase is:
> used cars

This can lead to showing up for all of the below searches:
> Japanese used cars
> Used car dealers

German used cars
Cars used for racing
Repo cars
Used trucks

Notice that it is a pretty broad match, and you probably do not want that. Use this match type only at the start of campaigns when you have low search volume or competition. Try to use delimiters as much as possible so that you're laser focused.

Modifier broad match (Symbol: Plus Sign +)
Using this symbol will tell Google to show ads only when the modified term(s) is included in the search phrase. If you really have no idea how to tighten down your keywords, use this limiter as a start. So using:

+used +cars

Will only show your ads when people search for:

Used cars
Used German cars
Used lorries and cars

But not when people search for:

Pre-owned cars
Toyota vehicles
Used trucks

It is a lot tighter, and that's the way you want it to be.
See what are the keywords that converts well and worth keeping, and then quickly move on to using more specific match types.

Phrase match (Symbol: Quotation Marks " ")
Using the quotation marks will show your phrase as is , and it is a good way to start, because it gives highly targeted ads, meaning you will get much more specific traffic. It generates close variations of the phrase and serve your ads there as well. Also, when your exact

keyword will appear in bold when it matches someone's search term, which helps to attract the searcher's attention. This is also a good matching option ss you can't manually add bold text or other formatting to your ad text.

So using:

"used cars"

Will only show your ads when people search for:

Red **used cars**
Used cars dealers
Used cars parts

But not when people search for:

Used rental car
Used German cars
Used lorries

Exact match (Symbol: Square Brackets [ ])

Attempt to use square brackets as much possible, especially after you have tightened down which key words or phrases converts best. No variations are allowed to show your ads when you use exact match. When you have confirmed a keyword as a winner, design and split test specific landing pages so that you can continue to inch your conversions up.

Negative match (Symbol: Minus Sign -)

This will remove the modified term from the search. This is a very important modifier, as there are bound to be plenty of irrelevant matches, which you must cut and trim early on in your campaign. Failing to do this leads to costly campaigns with poor results.

ORGANIZING YOUR CAMPAIGN

1) Campaign - A Campaign as just a way to organize your advertisement into different groups. A single Google account can

have campaigns for different products or websites. Since testing is the key to lowering your cost per click, the way you organize your campaigns is very, very important. If you mix it up or lose track of what each campaign is supposed to contain, your tracking will become inaccurate, and you will become confused about the results that you get. If your ad is doing good, it should still make you money, but poor testing means it is more expensive than it actually should be

2) Ad groups – Ideally if you have 50 keywords, you should write 50 ads and track them in 50 different ad groups. However, this is not practical, so you will have to cluster similar keywords together in the same ad group and use the Split and Stick method introduced later in the chapter to maximize your time.

Each ad group should only be focused on one type of product or service. If they are highly related, that means they are just different versions of the same product, so it's fine.

You absolutely must not lump keywords for different products or services in a single ad group. It is wasteful and will definitely cost you more than it should have.

OPTIMIZING YOUR CAMPAIGN

Split Testing

You will need to treat Adwords as a marathon, rather than a sprint. To achieve a long term success on Adwords, you will always need to be split testing.

1) Search Advertisement Split Testing

Have 2 ads running at the same time, delete the inferior one and then try to beat your best again.

If fact, you should have wrote 50 ads before you even started, so that you can choose the best to start with, and start refining from there. Keep track of which works and which did not, because you might reuse your headlines and benefits in future campaigns and other media.

In order to be sure that the 2 ads that you test will have different long term results, use tool at www.splittester.com. It is based on statistical significance, where you need around 30 clicks to be sure that your results will differ over longer periods of time.

You will need to test each and every keyword or phrase to see which gives you the highest response rates

2) Landing Page Split Testing
Having 2 different pages for split testing is the other important factor contributing to the success of your marathon.

While split testing is important, do not get bogged down too much into the nitty-gritty if there are other forms of traffic you have not implemented. Get other forms of traffic done instead. As you start online advertising, getting all forms of traffic done up first are usually better use of your time, unless you are consistently spending upwards of $5,000 a month, where every additional 0.1% can mean a difference in thousands of dollars' worth of conversion.

In that case, you should probably find an expert in that field and outsource that, while you focus on other forms of more profitable business, like adding another revenue stream.

Split And Stick
Some keywords do well by themselves, and they will deserve their own ad group, which comes along with additional work such as doing landing page split test and also the search ad split test.

Yes, it takes additional work to test out the different landing pages and the search ad, but these are the important keywords that you should optimize to get maximal results.

Negative Keywords and Irrelevant Keywords
Some keywords just cost you clicks without turning into business, so you will have to find these keywords and remove them. For example, you do not want people who are searching for *free*. Hence, you can put a negative modifier like -free.

Some irrelevant keywords could include a brand slogan or lyrics of a song. Use -lyrics to cut it out.

DISPLAY ADVERTISING

There used to be lesser competition here, but as more advertisers enter the online advertising arena, more advertisers are looking into other sources of traffic, and display advertising is one of the additional source.

There are many proponents out there who says that display advertising are not as effective or profitable as search advertising, however that is not true. It might be true that it is more difficult to get good traffic however, only further testing can tell if the quality of traffic is worth purchasing.

The positive thing about display advertising is that the traffic is not as limited as search advertising, as there are always people surfing the web, but that they are not necessarily searching for your products or services.

As again, the key to achieving success in display advertising is to test different advertising images, in accordance with the rules in chapter 7.

Note that since testing is so important, it is important not to turn on display advertising in the AdWords campaign because it will mess up your results.

Set up another campaign for your display advertsing alone.

YOUTUBE

YouTube is also part of the Google display network, so you can also set up your campaign to run specifically on certain types of videos. There are a few types of advertisements that you can run on YouTube, which can all be controlled via your AdWords account.

Banner Display Advertisements can appear anywhere on the site except on the homepage.

In Display Advertising are ads for native YouTube videos that appear alongside other YouTube videos. They appear as suggested videos similar to the one that you were viewing. These appear more natural, as users are on YouTube to view content similar to what you are offering and the right audience are more likely to click in to view.

The below 3 types of advertisement are more intrusive, and hence can only be run when the owner of the video has given Google their permission to monetize their

In Video Overlay Advertisements are the small, long, transparent box overlaid on top of videos at the bottom

TrueView In Stream Advertising are skippable videos that can be inserted before, during or after the video

In Stream Advertising is another type of video advertising which usually appears before the video. The first 5 seconds are non-skippable, and hence if you do not intrigue the viewer enough, they will skip the rest of what your video has to offer.

However, the mechanics of In Stream Advertising is very different then when you use videos to build up trust and authority in your field, because you are interrupting the actual content that other people wants to watch.
Hence, it will need to grab the attention of your viewers by the throat right at the start, preferably within the first 5 seconds of the video.

Hence, to craft the video advertising, you will also need to stick to the rules of advertising as stated earlier in Chapter 7. When you are just starting out, you can start out with video sales letter, or the read and speak format which offers the lowest production cost, and thus likelier to net you higher returns at the outset.

You can have promotional videos as a more expensive choice of advertising because you will need to incur the video production costs, starting from around $5,000 upwards to tens of thousands of dollars. Also, if your video is not intriguing enough, people are likely to skip over to the content that they really want to watch after the 5 seconds.

RETARGETING ADVERTISING

It is actually very easy to set up a retargeting campaign, and you only have to set place a simple code in the website that you want to track. but note that you will need at least a 100 people in your audience list before it starts running, so don't panic if it does not start running right away. Here 2 tips for smart remarketers

Delayed Remarketing
Probably a 3 to 5 days delay would be a good guide, so that you can save your remarketing dollars on people who are going to buy anyway but wants to wait for their pay to come in a few days later or for any other reasons at all.

Impression Capping and Ad Frequency and rotation
You also do not want to reach a stage where your ads are absolutely everywhere all the time, because then it's only going to become intrusive and even potential customers may start to strike off your company from their consideration. Also, depending on your product, it might not be necessary to show your ads so many times in a day and hence it saves you money as well.

---

*
Action Time!

Log in using your Gmail address and create an AdWords account now! This is an absolutely essential for any marketer who wants to excel in their field, or to create a lean, mean marketing machine.
Definitely, it will seem intimidating at first due to the platform's immense customization capabilities, however, once you get the hang of it, you will be able to focus on the functions that are important to you right now.

~

CHAPTER 14:

FACEBOOK

There are so many figures on how many Facebook users are there, that I no longer know which are true and which are not. So I am not going to bore you with figures, but only that I want to tell you that Facebook Advertising is the **most powerful medium** right now, as of 2015 for you to do advertising for consumers.

It is slightly more difficult to target businesses, unless they are small businesses, which act much like typical consumers.

So why is it so powerful? Simply because it cost so little to reach so many TARGETED prospects. Comparing it with all other forms of advertising, Google included, Facebook is still the cheaper form of advertising.

Perhaps Facebook is now at where Google was 10 years ago, where clicks were so cheap anybody can make money with it with a decent amount of skill, or perhaps it will stay this way forever. Nonetheless, you should take advantage of it now, lest the price goes up, and we as marketers will lose out.

It is really easy to set up your Facebook advertising account and Page for your business or yourself. It really only takes less than 1 day to get started on Facebook, so this is the absolutely the 2nd item on your Action List, right after you have set up your website. If you need a guide on how to set up your own self-hosted website, check out the Radiation Marketing Silver Member's area for a quick step by step guide to churning out your profit oriented website.

FACEBOOK RESEARCH

Follow.net
Sign up for a free account
Write down 3 competitors and run each of them on www.Follow.net

1. Note Ad Spend
2. Note Ad Copy
3. Note Display Ads
4. Note Landing Pages

Examine this data and compare it to your own offer/pages to improve or craft your offer. Now you know what is working in your market

Facebook Graph Search
The purpose of using this graph search is for you to target and expand on the number of customers you can reach. Remember about angling the sales message to increase the affinity with your customers? This is a powerful way for you to find out their common likes and interests.

1. **People** who like *(insert topic or page)*
2. **Pages** liked by people who like *(insert topic or page)*
3. **Groups** joined by people who like *(insert topic or page)*
4. **Products** liked by people who like *(insert topic or page)*
5. **Interests** liked by people who like *(insert topic or page)*
6. **Posts** by people who like *(insert topic or page)*
7. **Pages** similar to *(insert page)*

FACEBOOK PAGE

The first thing you will need to do to get started on Facebook is to set up your Facebook page. After setting it up, remember to assign a specific URL to your Facebook page.

E.g. www.facebook.com/RadiationMarketing.

Then you can distribute this URL on all the advertising material that you use as an additional popular channel for people to engage you.

Here are a list of different ways that you can use Facebook or any other forms of social media.

1) Brand awareness and establishment
2) Check-in deals
3) Competitions
4) Corporate and social responsibility channel
5) Customer support and service
6) Rally support for a cause
7) Humanizing your brand
8) Generate leads
9) News distribution
10) Polling and product feedback
11) Product and events promotion
12) Research

This list is definitely not exhaustive, and in this book I will be focusing on generating leads, because the focus on this book is to increase your marketing prowess and sell more things.

LIKES IS NOT EVERYTHING

You should have already heard that getting more likes does not mean anything if your purpose for being on Facebook is to sell more things. This is absolutely true. Hence, if you do want to get some likes before launching your promotion campaigns, get the likes as cheaply as possible. This means including other countries as well as those with different interests from your targeted groups. It does not matter even if the users are unlikely to ever purchase your products, because they are 3-5x more likely to 'Like' anything that they see. Note that these users will not be useful in engaging your content, but merely there as a confidence booster for actual potential clients.

If you do want potential clients to engage your content, then you should post useful content for prospects to download in order to start building your email list or promotions that are compelling enough for users to directly buy.

THE MOST POWERFUL FACEBOOK STRATEGY

Now most of the time, people will tell you that if you want to get conversions on Facebook you have got to use the Website Conversion options on Facebook Advertising. However, that is not true. The reason is that if you do choose that option, the placement of the ad copy and pictures are just insufficient for people to quickly find out more. Hence, you would be a lot better served by creating a post, with 1 or 2 pictures, and lots of text descriptions. Then, add a link to your promotion page, and this will probably double or triple your conversion rates.

The simple reason is that you can provide more information about your products and services and then craft compelling offers so that people will want to find out more, and then click into your website. Also, the picture that you are allowed to put up in your ad is also much bigger, and hence more effective at capturing the audience's attention. When you are dealing with so many people who will be looking at your advertisement, all these small improvements in conversions makes a huge difference.

As again, for what to actually post on your Facebook, you may refer to the guidelines, as set out in Chapter 6 and 7, which forms the basis for creating your advertisements.

This is also maximizes returns for your time spent, as the people who are responding to you are all potential buyers, and not people who are just looking around. These means you do not need an entire Social Media department, where you are unable to justify the cost benefits equation.

All your advertisement design should adhere strictly to the guidelines in Chapter 7, which forms the core of my unique Radiation Marketing Method. Hence, do not focus on the appearance, but only the contents within each point for maximum effectiveness.

And that is all you really need to know about Facebook, because just this one strategy alone is enough to greatly increase your sales. However, the trick here is crafting and refining a compelling message and having a great offer that converts well.

TARGETING

At first you might think that reaching all of the people in your target age group is your best bet, but this is definitely not true. You should only choose and pick the most responsive potential customers to target, so that you can make your $50 worth of traffic feel like $500 worth of clicks.

CONVERSIONS

Definitely you will need to measure your returns on the amount of money you are putting into Facebook. It might not seem like much, paying only $50 to reach 10,000 targeted customers in a day, but if you do this over a month, you are essentially spending $1,500 for the entire month of 30 days. Hence, you must be able to justify the amount spent to get that 1 new customers.

At this point, you should already have your CPS, CPL, LCV and ATV at your fingertips, because if you do not yet know what it is, please go and download the Radiation Marketing Action Plan and start working on the numbers. As I have mentioned, this book is a Blueprint, it teaches you how to build something, so if you are not going to do it, then this knowledge is not going to be helpful to you, and I do not want to waste your time learning something that you are not going to use. So finish up that Marketing Action Plan now! So if you have already finished the MAP, please bear with my incessant rant, because I really want you to gain real value from the time that you invested in reading this book.

So you should also know what the CTP is per new customer, and this is the maximum amount you should spend for each customer. Of course there are some customers that goes on to purchase other things, and hence worth more than the ATV you calculated, but for a start, always be on the safe side, and assume that the amount they spent is the only amount that they are ever going to spend.

Assuming your ATV is $50, and the CTP is $10, every day you will need to get around 5 customers from the Facebook advertisement if you were to be profitable. Now 5 customers a day might seem like a lot, but in the education industry, I can usually get 5 prospects on a $30 daily budget. Hence, you should have some leeway to work with, even if you do not have very profitable advertisements as yet. Do not worry, you just have to refine, test and improve, and eventually your conversion rates will go up, as cost decreases accordingly

WHO SHOULD USE FACEBOOK?

This strategy is not for everyone though. If you are doing B2C sales, then this is a very powerful strategy. Of course, this might not be that suitable for large businesses or fast moving consumer goods, but there are definitely ways to tweak this strategy for it to work.
Also, there are certain businesses that might seem like a mix of B2B and B2C, then in this case, I think you should most definitely try. Facebook traffic is cheap and fast and easy to test, and it is highly likely you are able to profit from it. However, if you are doing B2B sales, then you will might need to use Google Adwords, because of its specificity, or LinkedIn, because of its business nature.

> * **Action Time!**
> Create a Facebook account for either you, or a separate one for the company. Then create a Page for your company and start including the unique link in all your marketing collaterals, including your email signature. Then watch the customers roll in as you start your advertisements!

CHAPTER 15:

LINKEDIN

LinkedIn - The largest professional network around. This is excellent if you are selling to big businesses because you can get the links to send direct and targeted messages to selected people who call the shots. LinkedIn started out mainly as a recruitment resource, where professionals could share their knowledge and expertise. It has evolved a lot over time and now it is a lot more than that.

There are two ways you can use LinkedIn. One is for networking, where you can start building up your subject matter expertise by answering questions in the forums, or by starting groups and posting interesting and provocative questions. This is a good way to start building up equity so as to reach a point where you start getting free, consistent and good quality leads. Provided you have the luxury of time.

Most of the times when business owners approach me, they want to sell something – FAST. So the networking aspect is usually not what I offer my clients, because it is slower. Saying this, networking does not cost you much other than your time, so doing both concurrently is what I would suggest.

I jump into understanding their business and start crafting compelling messages to advertise on LinkedIn so that I can acquire good quality leads within a couple of weeks. You can do that too, if you put in enough time to learn about understanding your customer and what they really need. As again, refer to Part III of the book for the specifics on crafting compelling messages.

SETTING UP YOUR COMPANY PAGE

The very first thing you need to do when you want to start using LinkedIn for business is to set up your company page. There are a few pre-requisites however, as listed below.

1. You must set up a personal profile with your actual first and last name.
2. You must attain profile strength of either "Intermediate" or "All Star."
3. You must have several connections on your profile.
4. You're a current company employee and your position is listed in the "Experience" section on your profile.
5. You have a company email address added and confirmed on your LinkedIn account.
6. Your company's email domain is unique to the company.

SELF-SERVE ADVERTISEMENTS

Once the company page is done, you can start putting up self-serve advertisements. LinkedIn advertising is profile-based, compared with the interest-based advertising used in Facebook. One trick to lower the cost of your Facebook Ads is to be more targeted. As the profile of your audience gets more specific in Facebook, your CPC should drop, as the right audience are more likely to click. However, the effect is reversed on LinkedIn. As you add more profile filters, meaning that as the number of profiles decreases, the cost actually increases.

LinkedIn campaigns do not come cheap. Typically, there is a minimum charge of US$2 for Cost-Per-Click (CPC) campaigns. As more filters are applied, the cost per click increases as the campaign is more targeted. For example, a generic campaign targeting the whole Singapore LinkedIn community of 1.15m members would have an average bid price of US$3.23 vs the average bid price of US$4.44 for a campaign targeting IT professionals of large Enterprises would have an but targeted at just 5,000+ members. If you change the audience from Singapore to US, that would easily increase to beyond US$5 CPC, as there are more advertisers in US than in Singapore.

This is where you want to start out, so that you can start refining your messages so that they are compelling enough for you to justify using the more expensive Display Advertising, which requires a quarterly budget of $5,000.

DISPLAY ADVERTISING

To start using display advertising, you will need to set aside a decent budget quarterly budget of $5,000 if you want the LinkedIn advertising team to contact you. You can't do this yourself. To decide if this is for you, you have to look at your cost per customer and what is you conversion ratio. The higher your conversion ratio, the higher chance this will succeed for you.

As mentioned, it will be good to start crafting and refining your messages so that your messages can work on a smaller scale first, before you scale it up and put more budget into it. This will ensure that you get good ROI on the amount you put in. There is no point in gambling on big amounts, when you can use smaller amounts to test first.

TARGETING OPTIONS

Here we are back to setting up our ideal customer profile. In marketing, it's always about reaching the right people.

Do they have specific job functions?
Do they have certain skills?
Where are they located?
Do they work in a certain industry?
Do they belong to certain LinkedIn Groups?

These are the various targeting options that LinkedIn allows you to choose from. It is very powerful as you can specifically target those who are of a specific seniority and can make the buying decision.

- Geography
- Company name
- Industry

- Company size
- Job Title
- Job function
- Seniority
- School
- Skills
- Age
- Gender
- Groups

The standard landing page should have a video sales letter by one of the best consultant in the company, who achieves the top sales consistently. This person should already know the customer well, and you need to multiply his or her sales efficiency by using a media to scale it up. Landing pages with both video and a download usually works the best. It's fine even if it is an animated PowerPoint Presentation with voice over.

NETWORKING

Once you have reached out to them, networking is what you will need to close the sale. In this internet era, all larger B2B sales in Singapore will require networking to complete. Of course, for the older generation business owners, they might not speak English and have already built up their network. You are unlikely to find them on linked in, but you can definitely find their C-suite executives if the business is large enough.

If you are targeting smaller businesses, where they are yet to have a presence on LinkedIn, then you can look for other sources, for example industry directory listing where you can find their email. A good place to start will be the DP Bureau in Singapore, where most businesses are listed or the Times Directory of Businesses (aka Buku Merah) if you are in the B2B industry.

You can also just call the company and ask to speak to the in-charge of whatever department you want to speak to, although it will be more difficult, as you do not have access to that person's background or connections before you talk to them. It is definitely easier to speak to them if you understand more about them.

Obviously, such smaller businesses are not suitable for marketing via LinkedIn, because of the smaller size, so reaching them via direct email or call will be more effective. Of course, you will still need to have a compelling message when you do reach out to them.

Assuming you can find them on LinkedIn, the best way to reach out to them is via a premium profile. If you own a business, you should be able to at least swing a few hundred dollars a year for such a powerful networking tool. Premium profiles get a lot more views, and hence exposure for your company, and it also gives you access to lots of tools to quickly build up a large number of connection even if you are a complete newbie on LinkedIn. One of them is the "Open Networker", where you can reach out to connect to people who are also interested in building up their connections.

Premium Accounts basically offer you the below privileges.
- See more profiles when you search
- Adding filters to your searches to make the results more targeted
- View a full list of those who have viewed your profile
- Send InMails – Direct emails to the LinkedIn users' primary email

Premium Account is a powerful leveraging tool if you are able to use it well. As this book focuses on sales and marketing, we shall look at the 2 types of premium account that they offer for this purpose, the Business Plus and the Sales Navigator. The other 2 premium account they offer is for job seekers and recruiters.

Incidentally, when you take a deeper look, hiring employees and finding customers are very similar. They need to fulfill similar criteria and characteristics before they have a good chance of fitting in with your company, whether as an employee or as a customers. And this is the power of LinkedIn for sales and marketing purposes.

LINKEDIN BUSINESS PLUS

The Business Plus is likely the best overall option for most of your general networking needs. You will have additional access to a wide variety of visibility, reach, and search tools. Just a few months back there were three different types of plans: Business, Business Plus, and Executive. Now it is simplified into 1 Business Plus Plan.

LINKEDIN SALES NAVIGATOR

Uniquely situated for B2B selling, where trust and recommendation via social networks is vitally important for sales to occur – The LinkedIn Sales Navigator, the tool you need for the era of social selling.

There are features like lead recommendation by account, news mentions, and account recommendation. The idea, basically, is to give you up-to-date information from LinkedIn about potential leads.

When it comes to business-to-business sales, the old system of cold calling is increasingly ineffective. Even if buyers do not say, but they feel, "I want you to find me if I'm the right person; I want you to be informed about me; I want you to go in through a warm introduction." This helps buyers to save time, a much valued commodity they would rather spend elsewhere.

Social selling consists of four main steps:
1. Establishing a presence
2. Finding the right people
3. Engaging with those people
4. Building trust.

Essentially it still all comes down to building trust, and the Sales Navigator tries to cover all four points. It will recommend the sales leads you should be connecting with on the site, allow you to track updates and news related to important leads and companies and find mutual connections, including those in your company who can introduce you. It also allows updates on who your team has already contacted, and hence everyone can be kept updated on the progress status of each project. Each plan also grants you access to the Lead Builder, which lets you create lead lists with custom criteria to source and close deals.

LinkedIn Sales Navigator integrates well with Salesforce, so if you are already using it, so much the better.

LINKEDIN SEARCH

Now, if you are still not convinced of the value of LinkedIn, here's a few more reasons. While LinkedIn has a few premium options, they offer more or less similar features, one of them is the power of the advanced search and filtering options. LinkedIn Premium's main revenue source is via granting search and access to its member profiles as far as a totally unconnected linked in member, although this powerful privilege comes at the most expensive of the Premium option, the Recruiter Plan, usually used by HR companies.

If you combine this advanced targeted search with InMail, then you have the perfect B2B selling platform.

INMAIL

These are basically emails that are sent to user's primary email, as well as towards their LinkedIn inbox which they will see when they login to their LinkedIn accounts. One beauty of InMails, is that you are guaranteed a reply within 7 days, or the InMail credit is returned to you. Also, even if the credit is returned to you, the user can still reply to that same InMail that you have sent.

This means guaranteed connection with a few new people every week! If you have something valuable to offer, this kind of networking speed is a surefire way to start getting your products and services out there to people who needs it.

I also encourage you to read through some of the case studies from LinkedIn's customers. Here, you'll also learn more about how major brands and recruitment firms achieved their goals with the help of LinkedIn Premium.

---

*   # Action Time!

If you do not already have a presence on LinkedIn, you are missing out! Create your personal LinkedIn account and then another one for your company, if you have one.

Your personal account will need to have a reasonable number of connections before you can set up your company profile, so get started now!   ~

CHAPTER 16:

TWITTER

Remember the times when you had to go out to networking events to "press the flesh". After meeting people who wants to sell you things again and again. You think to yourself, "There must be a better way!"

Welcome to Twitter. Informal networking supercharged. You save on travel and transport time, and you only get to meet targeted leads whom you know you want to work with. Of course, your target group has got to be using Twitter in the 1st place.

The good thing about twitter is that you can interact quite a lot with the people whom you meet here, because successful Twitter users are all responsive, and so you can start to build trust at the speed and efficiency of the internet age.

However, unlike paid advertising, where you can offer lead generation promotions off the bat, all networking events takes time. People do not like sale-sy networkers, so it will definitely take longer than paid advertising, ranging between 30 days to 6 month before you can build up a significant number of followers.

Of course, this is not the only way to use Twitter, I have listed quite a number of uses of social media in Chapter 14, and they are all applicable here. However, as our focus is on Marketing and Sales, the best way to use Twitter is to use it as a networking platform.

REALTIME INTERFACE

Twitter's power is in its highly connective real time interface, and there has been a seismic shift away from mundane everyday life tweets to useful and compelling information-rich tweets.

This also facilitates the use of Twitter for use as a Customer Service platform. As business owners, you can conduct real time market research to help you understand more about your target market and hence come up with new features and designs that people wants. To be fair, Singapore does not have that much Twitter users, however, you can still glean insights from the tweets in other countries as well. Furthermore, this might help you to stay ahead of the curve as well!

HUMANIZING THE BRAND

People do business with people and Twitter provides a perfect vehicle for businesses to showcase the people behind the brand. This person could be the founder, or CEO or the business 'celebrity' that customers are familiar with.

This provides a more human channel for the customers to connect with, and it also helps them feel that there is someplace where they can let their thoughts be known, which is increasingly important to customers in this new era.

TARGETED FOLLOWING

While Twitter is a social network, using it for a business purpose means that you should use it specific to your business needs, via targeting. If you do not follow anyone and do not have a following, Twitter is just an empty shell. So who should you start following?

- People whom you can follow
- Similar celebrities in your profession
- Profession or industry press or journalists
- People looking or likely to buy your products and services

- People talking about and/or looking for advise in your industry
- Complimentary industry professional or customers

Now just because you follow them does not mean that they will follow you back, and that's ok. The purpose is for you to start building up your network, so that you can start to gain some exposure.

GETTING FOLLOWERS

1) Retweeting
This is a useful method for you to alert a follower that you have shared their content, prompting them to check you out, and possibly follow you.

2) @ Mentions
For example, if someone tweets @MikeVectra Thanks I really enjoyed your book! Even I am not following the person, I can still see that I have been mentioned in a post, and I might check it out, and start following that person

3) Promoting your @ handle
You can place your handle name everywhere on your advertising material so that people can start to follow you if they are interested in your content. Email signatures, brochures, websites are a few examples.

TWEETS

Here are a few rules that you should absolutely stick to when using Twitter for business purposes. You must ALWAYS have:
1. Selective Connections
2. Meaningful Content
3. Genuine Helpfulness

Here are some more specific events:

- An observation
- An interesting book, webpage or video
- An event you will be attending
- Your own content
- Someone else's content (Blog, video or article)
- Chatting with people, questioning and answering
- Retweets

HASHTAGS

This helps unrelated people listen in and respond to a specific topic that they are interested about, otherwise everyone will have to follow each other to do that.

Mashtagging means to attach an unnecessary or unrelated number or tags to your tweets. A word of warning if you are thinking about this, because if you attempt to piggyback on unrelated hashtags, especially those of other brands, you will get reported, and your account might even get banned. Hence before promoting a hash tag, make sure that it is unique so that you can claim it as your own and start to use it.

TWITTER LISTS

You should want to get on as many related lists as possible, because in a content rich channel like Twitter, lists help people to sift through the noise, to find what they are looking for. In order to get on other lists, the only way is to become a provider of good content. Nowadays, content is not only king. Content is Cash.

So the above are a few ways for you jumpstart your Twitter account. Patience is absolutely essential, so stick to a one hour a day for 30 days, and if you are doing it right, you should start to have some minor results. Given that it only costs you your time, your networking efforts should be profitable within 3 months.

"SO THERE ARE 4 PLATFORMS. WHERE DO I START?"

Assuming you start off all the 4 platforms from scratch, Twitter is probably the slower way to connect with your customers, so I would highly starting on other platforms (Facebook, then LinkedIn, then Google) before embarking on Twitter.

By starting, I do not mean to have a massive presence already before moving on to the next platform. At least have a basic company page, and start to use some of the advertisement features so that you can have gauge actual response for you to use as a reference point. This means, you should be able to establish a presence on all 4 platforms within a week, if you are not so involved in the day to day operations.

---

* **Action Time!**

Create a Twitter account and start following the right people. You do not need to spend much time, limit it to a maximum of 1 hour a day, and you will have a powerful presence before you know it!

~

CHAPTER 17:

THE LIMITLESS TRAFFIC PROTOCOL

When your conversion rate is at a phenomenal percentage, you can then slowly expand into other more expensive traffic sources such as offline avenues.

As again you definitely need to start testing, starting with 2 or even 3 ads. Your previous winning ads should come in handy, as what might not have worked as well on other media might be super effective on the current medium.

It is unwise to rely exclusively on Adwords, Facebook, email or any single source of traffic and marketing purposes, so as you grow, you must expand and diversify. Each source of traffic only represent a fraction of the total amount of customers that you can get. The problem is that the other traffic sources costs more to reach than via online methods, so they might not be so profitable at the start.

Hence, I always recommend starting with online advertising to get a feel of what works best, then max out its conversion ratio before moving it to offline platforms, so that you have a much greater chance of success.

The greatest strength of online advertising is its cost and speed, but this is also its greatest weakness. You can reach out quickly to many people, but its rules and Terms of Use can change as suddenly as the weather. It is not unheard of that many businesses were booming with business one day, and then cold as ice the next. So while it is ok to start out focusing and mastering exclusively 1 form of traffic first, it is definitely not wise to continue to rely on that traffic source just because it has been working out so well for you.

You MUST diversify, once you are able to.

Ok so now that you have various methods to get traffic, which ones should you start first? The best way would be to start from the cheapest sources, which I have found out to be in the below order. Starting with the cheapest from of traffic means that you have lots of leeway to improve your conversion ratio. Cheap traffic means that you can be profitable even if your conversion rate is low. From there, you can and should increase your conversion rate so that you can be more confident of using expensive traffic profitably.

1) Facebook / LinkedIn / Google Adwords
2) SEO
3) Other online PPCs methods such as the display network
4) Email Promotions
5) Social Media Networking
6) Affiliates
7) Direct Mail
8) Banner Ads and Ad Networks
9) Press Releases
10) Print Advertising, TV and Radio

Items 2 to 10 are more expensive and less controllable than the media higher in the above list, and that's why I recommend starting in this order. Note that it is likely that you might not even need to go beyond the first 5 sources of traffic, because you are already overwhelmed by customers.

And this is how the Limitless Traffic Protocol works.
1. Start with the cheapest form of traffic so that you can convert profitably.
2. Test and improve the conversion percentage
3. Move on to the next level of traffic
4. Once you can convert point number 7 onwards profitably, you would truly have an unlimited amount of traffic. Not only that, you will be able to get free branding and publicity equity too!

SALESPEOPLE, RESELLERS, AFFILIATES, DISTRIBUTORS AND CHANNEL PARTNERS

Whatever they are called in your industry, the rule is always the same: "They should **never** be your testing ground for your marketing or sales."

You must only give them working parts of your funnel to send out to their customers. This can be an extremely profitable relationships if they can benefit from their partnership with you, but if it bombs, it is almost impossible to recover. Make sure whatever you give them works, and that they only get happy and satisfied customers.

It is the same with your salespeople, because they are with you more for the commission than anything else. Give them something that works, and they will be happy to stay, making you profits many times over its cost.

KEY TO PROFITABLE TRAFFIC

You will need to test repeatedly, to continually improve on what is working. Businesses in your industry are also constantly changing and improving so the only way to stay ahead of the pack is to improve faster than they are.

It is really not all hype when I talk about improvements at 2X, 4X 16X or even 100X. Continual testing and improvement will definitely bring about such an improvement. To get there quickly, you will not only have to test fast, but to eliminate quickly as well.

PART V: APPLICATION

Congratulations on reaching the last part of this book. If you have skipped to this last part of the book to get your Action Guides and Gold Membership, you probably have some knowledge about marketing and or you just want to get started NOW, and good for you! Here's the link to get started if you have not received your Gold Membership login details:

www.rmvic.com/gmd-sysblu-rms

Any action beats inaction, because as you try to do something, you start to meet obstacles along the way. This is good, because as you overcome these obstacles, slowly, but surely, you will gain more clarity.

Saying that, sometimes it's better to take some action slowly, rather than massive action. Especially when there's money involved. Because you can lose money really, really fast.

But if it does not cost you anything other than your time, go full steam ahead and do it!

In the next 2 chapters, I will discuss more about the application of all that I have said so far. Everyone has the same 24 hours in a day, and it is not only about getting more things done, but also about getting the right things done. This is discussed in Chapter 18, and in Chapter 19, I will talk about the fundamental reasons why people succeed and some people do not.

CHAPTER 18:

TIME MANAGEMENT

There are also many business owners I have met who tells me that they do not have time to set up such complex automated systems. Of course, this is good for me, and that's why my business is thriving with helping business owners set up their Marketing Systems.

However, time can always be found and multiplied if you want to find a way to do it. How else can so many business owners be free of their business to pursue the dreams they worked so hard for?

As an entrepreneur myself, we are our own bosses and it's very easy to slack off and not do additional productive work to keep the business growing. A lot of this actually boils down to self-discipline, with which you can conquer the world. So how can we improve self-discipline so that we can manage our time better? Measurement is key. As an aside, just by measuring certain important numbers, the effectiveness and efficiency will naturally improve, simply because there is more clarity. Let's start with your Hourly Earnings Target.

CALCULATING YOUR HOURLY EARNINGS TARGET

Let's use the below example, based on some simple assumptions:
I want to earn $200,000 per year and that I only work 2000 hours in a year, and I am productive half the time.
2000 hours is based on the fact that we have 52 weeks in a year

and 11 gazetted public holidays according to our (Singapore's) Ministry of Manpower. So 104 days are weekends and 11 days are public holidays, so that leaves us with 250 days out of the 365 days a year, and assuming you work 8 hours a day, that will give you 2,000 hours a year .

Being productive half the time will give me a Productive vs. Non Productive (PNP) multiple of 0.5.

Yearly Earning Target	$ 200,000.00
Divided by Work Hours in a Year	2000 hours
Base Hourly Number	$100
Divided by PNP Multiple	0.5
Value Per Hour	$200

So now that you know your targeted value per hour, you can think about the below points:

Am I earning this amount per hour?

What are the tasks I can and should delegate to others?

What are the tasks that I should be focusing on to generate this amount of value per hour?

What tasks can I do to get a higher rate than this? (Refer to the Core Formulas for a guide)

Do I want to put in more time to increase my yearly earning target?

How can I increase my productivity multiple so that you can work less?

DELEGATING AND REPLACING YOURSELF

As an entrepreneur, you are usually overpaid to do some of the things you are doing now for your company (such as basic data entry), and also grossly underpaid for some of the other things you do (such as devising future marketing plans or upcoming product lines). Hence, you will need to find the things that are not worth your time doing, and delegate it to other people to do.

Running a business is not about doing everything yourself. It's all about delegating, and to go one step further, trying to replace yourself, while providing the same excellent product or service that you are providing. That is why having systems in place is so important. Naturally, this includes training systems, to increase efficiency in staff training is so important. People come and go, but you cannot and should not be doing the same training over and over again. It is simply a mindless waste of time, and hence if you do not have videos to train your staff, it's time to start implementing it now.

While your staff may not be able to perform every tasks perfectly as you would like them to, but you must remember that it's ok. There are certain tasks where good enough is good enough. For example, your staff might not make deliver goods as fast as you can, because you are more familiar with the area and you love driving, and hence can do this task faster. But at the end of the day, if it is still within the delivery timeframe that is promised to your customer, then all is good. And you should keep your hands off. Focus on the more profitable tasks instead.

THE TIME THIEVES' TRICK BAG

Do you know of those people who like to sit around, talking to colleagues during work time? I hope you are not guilty of being a time thief yourself, because you are robbing yourself off plenty of opportunities for making money.

Small talk about anything and everything happening to you and the world is endless, and cannot be less productive. You must reduce this as well as interactions with those who like to engage in such activity. It not only saps your time, but reduces your motivation to work as well.

If you are not spending your time wisely, you are wasting an amount equivalent to your base hourly rate.

Below are some of the common tricks that time thieves like to use, and how you can defend yourself against them.

1) **Innocent Question Trick**

   The inconspicuous "Have you got a minute?" quickly disarms many, who stops to answer, "Sure, what is it about?". They then go into lots of questions about small things, which you are sure they will be able to figure out had they spend a little more time thinking and searching on the web. There are other types of "innocent questions", hence do not be fooled by the other variations as well.

Your Time Defense Measure:

"I'm really busy right now, but I would be able to spare 15 minutes at 4pm. Let's tackle all the problems that you might have then."

This sends out the message that you do not want to spend unnecessary time talking, but not in a unfriendly way. An excellent way to maximize productivity.

2) Meeting Trick

Meetings are a crazy waste of time. If you absolutely have to, it would be good to have some escape plans in place so that you are only in the meetings when you need to be.

If you are the one conducting the meeting, you should consider, would it be better to do away with it altogether? Perhaps you can circulate a memo, or perhaps a stand up meeting is all you will need.

Your Time Defense Measure:

If you are required to attend meetings: You must prepare in advance what information you will need to contribute, and do it with a prepared, minimum time, maximum impact presentation. Also, have somebody ready to phone you, where you can then excuse yourself to return the important call, and hopefully not need to return

If you are conducting meetings: Set the meeting immediately before lunch, or near the end of the day, where most time thieves are ready to go home, and hence will try their very best to be effective and productive.

a) Do not serve refreshments
b) Have a written agenda circulated in advance
c) Have and communicate a clear achievable objective for the meeting.

3) Trivia Trick

Time thieves using this trick will stop by to tell you any facts they just read about to start a conversation and escape the work they are supposed to do. Perhaps it's about the latest movie in the cinema, or perhaps it's about a certain singer that just died. Either way, it is irrelevant and non-productive

Your Time Defense Measure:

"I'm really busy right now, why don't we fix a time after work to chat?" Again, this impresses upon others the significance you place on time, without being curt. Most likely, you would not have to meet them after work anyway, because it's not that they want to talk to you, rather, they want to escape from work.

4) Soap-Opera Trick

Soap opera also draws people's attention unwittingly. And it is because of this that time thieves like to dramatize the things both in and out of the workplace. One example is that they like to talk to themselves about things like, "Oh how can I forget to bring that thing home?" or "What am I doing right now?". You must be thinking why are you even bringing up points that are irrelevant and only make themselves look stupid? I don't know, but the time thieves have already unknowingly stole 5 to 10 seconds of your time, and that is if you are disciplined enough to pull yourself back to work immediately. If you were foolish enough to respond, you will easily lose 10 to 15 minutes of your life each time it happens. And there are probably 6 daily episodes, more if you are willing to indulge. Say goodbye to an hour every day.

Your Time Defense Measure:

Discipline! You must be focused on your work enough to shut out all the external, unrelated influences. Ideally, you don't even notice such episodes, but if you do, quickly pull yourself back to your work. They usually would not expect you to respond, but if they switch to the "innocent question" trick, use the 1st measure introduced in point 1.

5) Other Tricks

There are so many other types and variations of tricks that time thieves can come up with, so you must get better at spotting them. Spot the tricks early, so that you can whip out your time defense measures quickly to guard your precious time. You might think all these are small matters and not really a big deal, since you also kind of enjoy talking to them, but let's put this into perspective. First, calculate all the hours stolen by the time thieves. Then make it more painful by multiplying the stolen time by your hourly rate. This should equate to them stealing upwards of a $100 from you every day. Is it worth that amount of money talking to them? I hope not. So stop doing it!

9 PRODUCTIVITY TECHNIQUES

1) Minimize meetings

Meetings take time to organize and usually contain items which are not relevant to all members. Furthermore, even if it does, it is usually more effective for a memo to be circulated, or postings on forums so that all relevant people are notified of any changes, and can act upon them while keeping others informed.

Meetings can also involve smaller number of people, so that it is more relevant for everyone.

2) Practice absolute punctuality

It is impossible to expect others to be punctual when you do not stick to your own timings. Effective people treasure their time, and prefers to do business with others who have similar traits. It is not uncommon to hear business owners say that they would not do business with suppliers and contractors simply because they are late for meetings.

If they cannot keep such simple appointments, imagine if they were given actual businesses, wouldn't it be logical to assume they are likely to be late in their delivery or unable to finish the given work on time?

It might be a bit tough minded, but such is how it works in the business world. Better to have an additional criteria and choose a better suppliers and business partners to work with.

3) Make and use lists

- Schedule
- To-do list
- To-call list

There are so many types of meeting planners and productivity tools, that just choosing a suitable one might send you reeling.

However, the magic is really in the **making and using** of the lists than which particular method or media that you use. Just start out with a simple lined notebook right away.

The difference between daydreaming and planning is whether you "think on paper". Just having a notebook to write down your thoughts and required actions greatly increases your effectiveness.

4) Fight to link everything to your goals.

The idea here is that as an entrepreneur, there really are many, many things that when you do will lead to increased income. But if you link them to your goals, you will be guided to do the more important activities first. Or you can also call it 80/20 prioritization. Do only the 20% of the things that will lead to 80% of the results. Or you want to simply it further, it's called working smart.

You have to ask yourself every day, every hour, every minute: "Am I doing something that is moving me measurably towards to my goals?"

You would need to have well defined goals for this to work, and then you will need to measure your performance and its contribution towards reaching your goal.

5) Plan and block off your time – Then stick to it!

This is the open secret that everyone knows about, but that nobody seems to get around to using it. You must have pre-specified activities for every time slot of your day, and you must make ABSOLUTE CERTAINTY to stick to it.

When you are just starting out, your estimation will be off and the activities from the first slot will spill into the next. You should stop doing the first and move on to the second item, making a mental note of the additional time required.

Over time, you will become excellent at planning and get a phenomenal amount of work done.

Here 2 reasons why many people do not use this technique

a) There is nothing to achieve as they did not set goals in the first place anyway. Little wonder that some people do not achieve much things.

b) They have a set of goals, but lack the discipline to plan their activities to maximize their time. As again, you can see here that even if you have the best plans and strategies for maximizing your time, nothing would work if you did not have the discipline to carry out the activities you have planned.

See the next chapter to improve your self-discipline.

6) Minimize unplanned activity

Such activities break off your momentum and can drag you far off tangent. For example, you sidetrack to do some quick research, but this drags you further and further into other things, and by the time you are back, you would have lost your momentum to perform your planned tasks.

Another example is a unexpected phone call (doesn't matter if it is a long or short call) that interrupts your thought, and you lose time simply to get back on track. Time lost this way is totally unproductive and uncalled for. It is your job to minimize such distractions.

7) Profit from "Barren" timings

These are the timings where you can only do some planned activities, but are usually left empty. For example, Driving and commuting timing is a great example of "barren" time. It is usually wasted, where you watch movies, play games or listen to latest pop songs to while away your time.

However, really successful people tries to profit from every bit of time they can scrape, something you can easily emulate. A marketing book or an audio program on marketing every time during this barren time will do wonders to boost your personal skills and discipline. I cover more on this secret technique to success in the next chapter.

8) Live Off Peak

This basically means do not go along with the crowd. Go to lunch a bit earlier, or a bit later, so that you do not waste time queuing along with other people to get your food. Avoid travelling, going to the bank, supermarket or post office at peak periods and you will likely save 5 to 10 minutes per trip. Added together, let's say you save 30 minutes a day, over a 250 workday per year, you gain an extra 125 hours of productive time. Going by 20 minutes per page, you would have written 375 pages, meaning you would have been able to finish a book just by using the time you have saved. Quite hefty, huh?

9) The Inner Game

At the end of the day, all the productivity techniques you have armed yourself with won't make a single bit of difference if you do not have the discipline to implement them. So it's all back down to self-discipline again. Do you have this strength of character to plan what you think and to do what you plan? Time management is really just a subset of self-discipline where you push yourself to use time in a much more profitable way. Of course, this will not come overnight, but start measuring and planning now, and you will reach your $10,000 per hour mark over time.

I'll be a bit blunt, but some people might need 2 lifetimes to achieve it, which means they will run out of time before they get there. How fast you get there is the key and it depends on how much self-discipline you can muster.

---

*   # Action Time!

Do you already own a **notebook or journal** which you can use to plan and think on paper? I have often found that this physical item is much better than a softcopy version, because it is much more accessible, but make sure it is small enough so that you bring it *everywhere* you go!   ~

CHAPTER 19:

SELF MOTIVATION

While I try to discipline myself to do more work, I find that I still end up slacking off more often than I would have liked.

However, I have found 1 superb trick to really get my engines started, and that is to start out your day with a video or book on your particular trade or industry, or any personal development and motivation audio programme, and this fuel will really get you through the entire day.

In my field of Online and Offline Marketing, there are really lots of new ideas and technologies that I have not yet explored, so I still have plenty of things to learn, and learning a little more about this topic on marketing each and every day keeps me really motivated to do more and more things faster and better!

In the previous chapter, I mentioned about the secret technique to success, and here it is: Listening to quality audio programs or audio books. This is the best way to start working on your goals, and it also keeps you absolutely focused and thinking about your goals.

Furthermore, it helps you to profit from time that would otherwise have been wasted, for example on your commute time to work. If you spend a total of 2 hours travelling to and from work, this will equate to an easy 500 hours of University Level education! A typical part-time 3 year private university program that you can take here in Singapore usually comprises of 4 modules per year, each consisting of 21 3-hour lectures. This will equate to a 252 hour program over 1 year.

So your University-on-Wheels would have provided you with twice as much knowledge than a typical year in a private university! These programs can be purchased cheaply, where you can listen to over and over again. A standard repertoire of a great audio program series would consist of those from Anthony Robbins, Brian Tracy, Jim Rohn, Tom Hopkins, Wayne Dyer and Zig Ziglar. Some of these programs can even be found on Youtube. Ah, the power of the internet!

If you have not read the famous book "Think and Grow Rich" by Napoleon Hill, then I would highly recommend it. For those who have already read it, you will know that the title itself summarizes the entire book.

Thinking about the specific steps to executing your business plan will help you to come up with more and more ideas and also keep your mind focused on *executing* your immediate short term goal.

Never mistake the title to involve only thinking about your dream, and expecting it to manifest in reality by itself. It may be possible, but really not what I'll recommend. What I meant is you must be constantly thinking of new ways to execute business strategies. As you think more about implementing the strategies, you will naturally be inclined to execute your plans, and it is this act of doing that will make you rich. The typical hardworking Singaporean works around 50 hours a week, but to join the ranks of the highly successful people earning more than $10,000 a month, you will need to put in between 60-70 hours a week. Or at least initially anyway. The tough part is getting yourself to actually *do* it.

FIND MORE REASONS

If you think back and realize that you are still where you were one year ago, you probably do not have enough reasons to succeed. Self-discipline is not easy to come by, and if you are lacking in that respect, you will need to find more reasons why you want to succeed.

Self-discipline is a function of motivation, of the reason(s) why you really, really want to succeed. You can't just have some material goals, rather you will need to attach strong emotional reasons as to why you want to achieve something. Different people have different reasons, and I bet you are curious what my motivation is.

For me, I would like to have the freedom from time and money, so that I can learn all the many, many exciting things that I am currently unable to do. And I would like to attain that freedom by helping people to achieve what they want to achieve. If you have watched the movie "Limitless", that is what I would like to become, less the drug of course. For now, learning to speak Japanese and also how to play the piano is top on my list.

If you do not yet have a wish-list of what you want to do, start one now! You can call this your bucket list, if you prefer, but that is limiting. It implies that is all there is, but it is not. It grows as you grow. Many internet marketer say that the money is in the list, and this is very, very true, for all sorts of lists. If you had a list of responsive customer, you can send out a promotion and get an instant cash surge. If you had a to-do list that you stick closely to, you will make much better use of time. If you had a list of products you can give to client, you will move your product much faster. If you benefits are listed, it helps prospects to decide faster that you have what they want.

Lists are just a more organized source of information that we absolutely need in our lives, and that you should start making better use of.

ACTION!

Massive action leads to massive results. The secret to success is really simple. It is merely doing what you need to do, all the time, whether you like it or not. If you are given 1 day to follow really successful people in one of their normal workday, you would probably think, "No wonder he is so successful. Look at everything he does!"

And that is also the reason why I try to include an "Action Time" section at the end of every chapter. You need to do before you can be and be before you can have. Action builds character, and character in turn builds wealth.

Some very successful people I know have this profound sense of dissatisfaction over their own performance, always thinking that they need to improve. I believe this is their way to discourage complacency and maintain peak performance, even when the stakes are the highest. This form of thinking helps to spur me to consistent action, even when I'm am tired and feel like taking a break. Because I know I have not achieved as much as I should have.

Everyone more or less knows what he or she needs to do in order to achieve more. Everyone also gets to doing it at some point in their life. So the real differentiating factor is: Who actually does it more often and in the most effective and efficient manner possible?

So to conclude this book, whoever has the most motivating reason(s) and the best coach (Note that a coach can refer to books, audio programs and video courses, of course, nothing beats a real life person giving you exact advice on what to do next in your specific situation), wins.

EVERYDAY VICTORIES AND SIGNATURE VICTORIES

One other technique I have found to be successful is that I keep a daily note of something important that I have learnt today, or in other words, the Victory of the Day. This has been a significant way for me to track my learning experience and daily reflections. As again, why is this so powerful is because it increases clarity of goals and the steps required to push yourself towards your Signature Victories.

Signature victories are those that people usually remember for life, and it is not measured in absolute amounts. For example one of them could be your first major consulting gig that pays off all your debt, and still leave you with plenty to spare for some nice things for you and your family.

Your next major gig could earn you twice as much, but it will not be as memorable as the one that removes all that heavy load off your shoulder, as you ascend to the next level in your life. Make time to celebrate these signature victories, so that you know all your hard work has paid off.

---

*   # Action Time!

Use your notebook to build a list of things you want to do. You can also download the **Radiation Goal Setting** Action Guide to help you along in your goal setting procedure. These goals will form the basis for working harder than others, because you want to achieve more than other people! People know what they have to do, but they always lack the motivation and the discipline to do it. Motivation gets you going, but habit gets you there. Make a discipline a habit and you will reach where you want to be, often sooner than you thought!   ~

MUST-KNOW RESOURCES

CREATING ADVERTISEMENT MESSAGES

Website
1. Image Editing: Paint.Net / Adobe Photoshop
2. Web Hosting: W3Hub (Singapore Based) / Bluehost (US Based)
3. Basic Website Construction: WordPress and the OptimisePress Theme or ProfitsTheme
4. Email Auto Responders: AWeber / GetResponse / MailChimp
5. Payment Gateway: Paypal / 1ShoppingCart
6. Online scheduling Software: vCita
7. Voucher Generation: RoboVoucher
8. Plays Audio on your website: http://audiogenerator.com/

Video Creation
9. Screen Recording: Camtasia / Screenflow
10. Video Creator: Explaindio Video Creator / Adobe After Effects
11. Purchase royalty-free soundtrack: www.audiojungle.com

Outsourcing the above
12. Purchase almost any online services: www.fiverr.com

ADVERTISEMENT PLATFORMS:

1. Google AdWords / YouTube
2. Facebook Ads Manager
3. LinkedIn Campaign Manager
4. Twitter

Do not be intimidated by the seemingly large number of tools that you have to learn. Break it down, and start from the most familiar ones that you know first. Everyone starts out not knowing anything, but as long as you are willing, it is easy to learn. There are screen recordings of all the above resources listed above, so learning by yourself is definitely not a problem.

I do not explain the resources here, because it's a list of lists that you should be aware of. There are plenty of instructional videos on the internet to learn more about the individual uses. Take a day to learn about 1 new resource and you would have finished the above list in a month's time.

Books and videos can only teach you about the tools for Business and Marketing, but only by actually doing it can you see how you can use the tools in creative and innovative ways to leapfrog over your competitors.

---

* **Action Time!**

Make a commitment to **start learning, one resource a day**, so that you at least know the basics of how each resource can help. Only when you know what solutions (and their corresponding cost) you would require for different situations, can you start to use them profitably!

~

ACKNOWLEDGEMENTS

I thank you for taking the time to finish reading the book and I hope you enjoyed reading it as much as I enjoyed writing it for you. It is organized to help you market and sell in the most effective and efficient way possible, and that's why I omitted much stories and examples, because I want it to be as close to a "How to" manual as possible.

I'm sure you do not see much stories in the manual that teaches people on how people set up their DVD player right? While there isn't much stories to illustrate my point, I want you to have absolute faith that it works. As long as you *start doing something* in the order I have mentioned, you will see results.

Books and videos can only teach you about the tools for Business and Marketing, but only by actually doing it can you see how you can use the tools in creative and innovative ways to leapfrog over your competitors!

ABOUT THE AUTHOR

Michael Vectra Tan grew up in a typical HDB Flat in the West area of Singapore. From young, he has read widely about motivation, business and success and frequently applied it to his work. He strongly believes in this statement:

"Motivation is the foundation, knowledge are the tools, and action is the key to success."

He is currently Chief Consultant at the company he founded, Radiation Marketing, where he helps companies and individuals alike to re-focus their priorities to build a Marketing System for maximal growth and profit.

Find out more about him at www.michaelvectratan.com